PLAN OF FIRST CLASS ACCOMMODATION.

WITHDRAWN

READING AND

WRITING ROOM

LOUNGE

ENTRANCE

PASSENGER ELEVATORS

BATH

BATH

LADIES

LAVT.

STEWARDESS

FEET FROM BOW

Rooms A 3 and 4 are fitted with 4 feet wide Bedstead (No. 1).

PRIVATE PROMENADE

PARLOUR SUITE

SETTING ROOM

BATH

STEWARDESS

LADIES LAVT.

ENTRANCE

PASSENGER ELEVATORS

BATH

GENTS LAV.

LADIES LAVATORY

BATH

195 FEET FROM BOW

SITTING ROOM

BATH

PARLOUR SUITE

PRIVATE PROMENADE

76, 77, 78, 81, 82, 83, 84, 87, 88, 89, 90 ARE FITTED WITH 4 FEET WIDE BEDSTEAD (NO. 1).

ROOMS — SUITE OF ROOMS — PARLOUR SUITE

WARDROBE ROOM

SITTING ROOM

BATH

STEWARDESS

LADIES LAVT.

ENTRANCE

PASSENGER ELEVATORS

STEWARDESS

BATH & WC

LADIES LAVT.

GENTS LAV.

BATH

PURSER

180 FEET FROM BOW

BATH & WC

ENQUIRY OFFICE

PURSERS OFFICE

SITTING ROOM

ROOMS — SUITE OF ROOMS — PARLOUR SUITE

92, 93, 94, 96, 98, 100, 102 ARE FITTED WITH 4 FEET WIDE BEDSTEAD (NO. 1).

eet above the Water Line.

DINING

RECEPTION

ARCHED OPENING

BATH

BATH

LADIES LAVT.

GENTS

ENTRANCE

PASSENGER ELEVATORS

STEWARDESS

SALOON

ROOM

ARCHED OPENING

180 FEET FROM BOW

ENTRANCE

PLAN

Deck A.

All Upper Berths (No. 2) in Rooms on this Deck are Pullman Berths and fold up.

Rooms A 5, 6, 7, 8, 9, 10, 11, 12, 14, 15, 16, 17, 18, 19, 20, 21, 22, 23, 24, 25, 26, 27, 28, 29, 30, 31, 32 and 33, are so fitted that a Sofa Berth for an extra passenger can be provided when required.

Rooms A 5, 6, 9, 10, 14, 15, 18, 19, 22, 23, 26, 27, 30 and 31, are lighted and ventilated from the Deck above (Boat Deck).

SITTING ROOM OF PARLOUR SUITE.

Deck—B.

All Upper Berths (No. 2) in Rooms on this Deck are Pullman Berths and fold up.

Rooms B 7, 8, 9, 10, 11, 12, 14, 15, 18, 19, 20, 21, 24, 25, 26, 27, 30, 31, 32, 33, 36, 37, 38 and 39, are so fitted that a Sofa Berth for an extra passenger can be provided when required.

STATEROOM B 21 AND SIMILAR.

Deck—C.

All Upper Berths (No. 2) in Rooms on this Deck are Pullman Berths and fold up.

Rooms C 1, 2, 3, 4, 5, 6, 45, 47, 49, 50, 51, 52, 53, 54, 56, 58, 60, 97, 103, 105, 107, 109, 111, 114, 116, 118, 122 and 124 are so fitted that a Pullman Upper Berth for an extra passenger can be provided when required.

Rooms C 40, 42, 44 and 46 are so fitted that a Sofa Berth for an extra passenger can be provided when required.

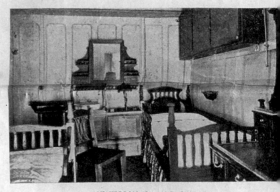

STATEROOM C 9 AND SIMILAR.
Showing Pullman Upper Berth closed.

Deck—D.

All Upper Berths (No. 2) in Rooms on this Deck are Pullman Berths and fold up.

Rooms D 40, 41, 42, 43, 44, 45, 46, 47, 48, 49 and 50 are so fitted that

Do

"Titanic
131428

Liverpool   2183

THE TRAGEDY THAT SHOOK THE WORLD

ONE CENTURY LATER

TITANIC

First page: A shipping register entry from April 10, 1912, logs the very first departure of the luxury liner *Titanic* from the port of Southampton, England, as she heads out on the initial leg of her only voyage. The ship would strike an iceberg and sink four days later. Todd Gipstein/Corbis

Pages 2–3: The RMS *Titanic* sails away from her final landfall in Queenstown, Ireland, on her maiden voyage across the Atlantic to New York City. She would not make it. Ralph White/Corbis

These pages: In a photograph taken in 1987, the *Titanic* rests on the ocean floor more than 12,000 feet below the surface of the North Atlantic. Woods Hole Oceanographic Institute

LIFE BOOKS

Managing Editor Robert Sullivan

Director of Photography
Barbara Baker Burrows

Creative Director Anke Stohlmann

Deputy Picture Editor Christina Lieberman

Copy Editors Parlan McGaw (Chief),
Barbara Gogan

Reporters Michelle DuPré (Chief), Marilyn Fu

Photo Associate Sarah Cates

Consulting Picture Editors Mimi Murphy (Rome),
Tala Skari (Paris)

Editorial Director Stephen Koepp

EDITORIAL OPERATIONS

Richard K. Prue (Director), Brian Fellows
(Manager), Keith Aurelio, Charlotte Coco,
Kevin Hart, Mert Kerimoglu, Rosalie Khan,
Patricia Koh, Marco Lau, Brian Mai, Po Fung
Ng, Rudi Papiri, Robert Pizaro, Barry Pribula,
Clara Renauro, Katy Saunders, Samantha
Schwendeman, Hia Tan, Vaune Trachtman

The editors of LIFE would like to specially
thank Art Braunschweiger, one of the team
of writers and editors behind the definitive
two-book series on the great ship's design,
construction and interior, *Titanic: The
Ship Magnificent.*

TIME HOME ENTERTAINMENT

Publisher Richard Fraiman

Vice President, Business Development & Strategy
Steven Sandonato

Executive Director, Marketing Services
Carol Pittard

Executive Director, Retail & Special Sales
Tom Mifsud

Executive Director, New Product Development
Peter Harper

Director, Bookazine Development & Marketing
Laura Adam

Publishing Director Joy Butts

Finance Director Glenn Buonocore

Assistant General Counsel Helen Wan

Assistant Director, Special Sales Ilene Schreider

Book Production Manager Suzanne Janso

Design & Prepress Manager Anne-Michelle Gallero

Brand Manager Roshni Patel

Special thanks: Christine Austin, Jeremy
Biloon, Jim Childs, Susan Chodakiewicz,
Rose Cirrincione, Jacqueline Fitzgerald,
Carrie Hertan, Christine Font, Jenna
Goldberg, Lauren Hall, Hillary Hirsch, Mona
Li, Amy Mangus, Robert Marasco, Kimberly
Marshall, Amy Migliaccio, Nina Mistry, Dave
Rozzelle, Adriana Tierno, Alex Voznesenskiy,
Vanessa Wu

Copyright © 2012 Time Home
Entertainment Inc.

Published by LIFE BOOKS, an imprint of
Time Home Entertainment Inc.
135 West 50th Street
New York, New York 10020

All rights reserved. No part of this book
may be reproduced in any form or by any
electronic or mechanical means, including
information storage and retrieval systems,
without permission in writing from the publisher, except by a reviewer, who may quote
brief passages in a review.

ISBN 13: 978-1-60320-213-8
ISBN 10: 1-60320-213-7
Library of Congress Control Number:
2011940198

"LIFE" is a registered trademark of Time Inc.

We welcome your comments and suggestions
about LIFE Books. Please write to us at:
LIFE Books
Attention: Book Editors
PO Box 11016
Des Moines, IA 50336-1016

If you would like to order any of our hardcover
Collector's Edition books, please call us at
1-800-327-6388. (Monday through Friday,
7:00 a.m.–8:00 p.m. or Saturday, 7:00 a.m.–
6:00 p.m. Central Time).

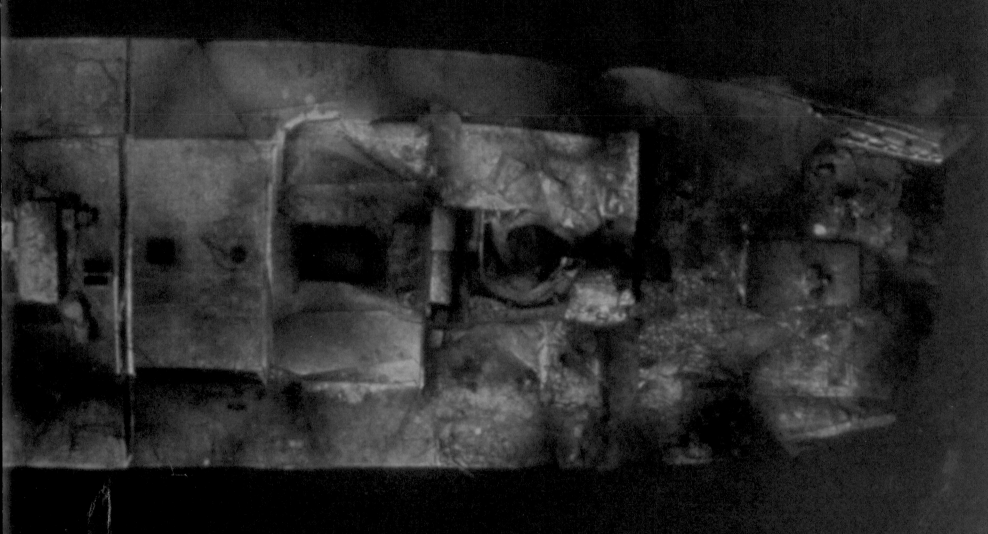

TITANIC

ONE HUNDRED YEARS ON

★

The passage of time causes a blue-gray haze to engulf, even hug horrors, and in rare instances, a disastrous tragedy takes on the sheen of romance, with a vague, diffuse sunshine breaking through the fog. This is true of the cataclysmic volcanoes that destroyed the Greek island of Santorini and the Italian city of Pompeii. They are regarded, today, much as we regard Plato's mythical Atlantis: as dazzling bygone civilizations dealt with by the deity in ways better rendered by poets than historians. Such is also true, thanks to Walter Lord, Robert Ballard, James Cameron and others (and, again, crucially, by the passage of, now, precisely 100 years) of the Titanic.

(Technically, the RMS Titanic, or just Titanic, but known by us all as the Titanic.)

Various elements made this drama essential: Had the great ship sunk on her second or third Atlantic crossing rather than her maiden voyage, had she been just marginally less grand, had Margaret "Molly" Brown or John Jacob Astor IV not been aboard, had the band not played as the frigid water rose, had the world been at war or otherwise distracted, well, the Titanic might be simply one more footnote in maritime lore. But as it is, the Titanic's is a legendary seafaring story to challenge Ahab and his Pequod.

Moby-Dick was, of course, a work of the

TOPICAL PRESS/GETTY

A massive 15-ton center anchor (above) destined for the Titanic makes its way in the spring of 1911 from a foundry in the Midlands of England to the local railway yard, whence it would be conveyed to Fleetwood on the coast, then across the Irish Sea to the Harland & Wolff shipyard in Belfast. Today this anchor—which was never deployed—sits in the well on Titanic's bow (opposite).

★

imagination (though certainly the *Pequod*'s ill fate was inspired by that of the tangible Nantucket whaler *Essex*). The *Titanic*, however, really existed, in steely magnificence and considerable tonnage, and her story is true. It actually happened.

It happened 100 years ago—April 14 and 15, 1912.

A century on, we return to this altogether extraordinary tale and parse the facts even as we rekindle the romance. Although many books have been written about the *Titanic*, it nevertheless surprised and delighted us at LIFE when we discovered how rich the photographic record was if we dug deep, finding gemlike rarities hidden among the always-seen and certainly indispensable pictures. We admit immediately: There is no extant photograph of the ship hitting the iceberg or sinking—only the renderings of artists—and you will not find one in the following pages. But you will learn the story of the Irish cleric and vocational photographer known to history as Father Browne, and you will sample his considerable (and expert) portfolio made while boarding and then sailing on the doomed ship. He was a far more immediate chronicler of the *Titanic* than Lord, Ballard or Cameron.

WALT DISNEY/EVERETT

Through Father Browne's work and contemporaneous journals, we return to the time. The Industrial Revolution and Edwardian Era had delivered the Western world to a juncture where anything was possible, and it's not inaccurate to view the *Titanic*, although the ship was strictly a commercial enterprise, as the Sputnik or Mercury program of her day. We were emboldened, we were energetic and we were shooting the moon. As we now know, with the sad but established history of the Space Shuttle disasters and *Apollo 13*, not everything goes as planned. The *Titanic* was declared unsinkable when she headed west into the Atlantic. And then . . .

And then the eternal tale unfolded, a tale recounted visually and in narrative in the pages that follow. Because of the *Titanic*'s durable hold on our imagination and our sense of romance, this is a contemporary as well as a hundred-year-old story. The latest photos from the bottom of the sea, where the *Titanic*'s final remains deteriorate even as you read these words, are in this book. And now, of course, at our local IMAX: James Cameron's upgraded version.

One hundred years later, we are all paying attention again. But then: We have never not paid attention. The astonishingly compelling story of the *Titanic* is perhaps the ultimate example of truth being stranger than—and certainly as riveting as—fiction. Heroes, villains, class warfare, survival, death, derring-do.

Turn the page and you'll see. You couldn't make this up.

THE
BUILDING

THE
BOARDING

he RMS *Titanic* was meant to make lots of money, not necessarily to foster any kind of societal benefit. She wasn't a massive dam that would send energy to the people in the valley below, and she certainly wasn't a mighty battleship that might serve to protect the homeland. She was a luxury passenger liner: the very best way in the world to move from here to there. Nonetheless, she caught the public's imagination even as she was being erected in a shipyard in northern Ireland (which was not, it is worth noting *Northern Ireland* with two capital letters; the *Titanic* was built a decade before the Irish Republic gained independence from Great Britain, and Belfast was just another British city "in the north" of one of the British Isles—not anything separate from Ireland, as Ireland then knew itself).

A strictly capitalistic enterprise, then, *Titanic* was touted as the best and the brightest, not to mention the biggest, and her legend grew even as she did. A cynic can view the liner as simply an earlier *QEII* or *Disney Dream* (with that cool plexiglass water slide that shoots you out over the shark-filled ocean), but she wasn't just that. Today, technology can do anything. In 1909, when work began in Belfast, technology could perhaps build the *Titanic*. The seeable limits of technology conjured a sense of wonder and possibility.

The boat was built in Belfast's Harland & Wolff shipyard, and although she was to be the latest star of Liverpool's White Star Line fleet, her Irish heritage ran deep. *Titanic*'s last port of call before heading west over the Atlantic was at Queenstown (now Cobh) in County Cork. The ship's designer was Thomas Andrews, who hailed from near Belfast, and yes, as James Cameron's movie correctly told it: Andrews was among the first to realize that *Titanic* was doomed after her encounter with the iceberg. There were many Irish aboard on April 15, most of them down below. Of those passengers in steerage, 113 had joined the ship at Queenstown, among them,

n the previous pages, White Star Line's superstars *Olympic* (left) and *Titanic*, sororal luxury liners, are afloat on the River Lagan in Belfast. At right, they are under construction at the Harland & Wolff shipyard, with *Titanic* at left. While the Royal Mail Steamer *Titanic* was ill-fated, the RMS *Olympic* would enjoy a long and illustrious career from 1911 to 1935, including service as an intrepid troop transport during World War I, earning her the nickname "Old Reliable."

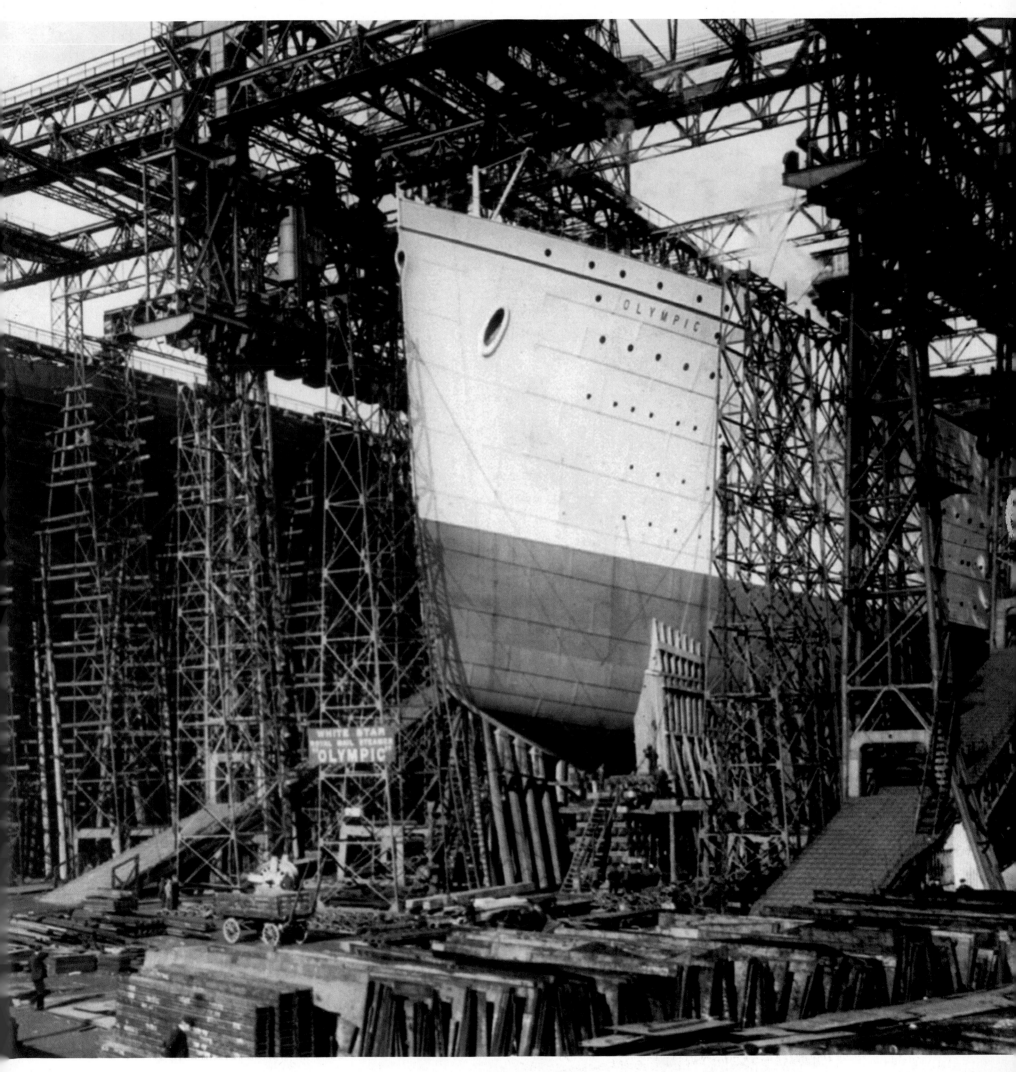

Bourkes, Connollys, Flynns, Foleys, Morans. Barely more than three dozen would survive.

Also among the rescued would be Lawrence Beesley, an Englishman, who would write one of the very first of scores—nay, hundreds—of published accounts about the tragedy, his entitled *The Loss of the SS Titanic*. In 1912, Beesley remembered in print, only two months after it had happened: "The last we saw of Europe was the Irish mountains dim and faint in the dropping darkness."

In July of 1907, the order was issued to begin work on two of the White Star Line's three planned sister ships, and the *Olympic* was given Harland & Wolff's yard number 400, the *Titanic* number 401. On *Titanic*, the gantry was nearly as long as three football fields. Ten cranes were used to raise large parts of the ship into position (more than 11,000 workers—a small city of workers—would toil on the *Titanic* before her maiden voyage). As the photograph on the pages previous implies, work began earlier on *Olympic*, and in fact she launched earlier, in 1910, and entered service in 1911 (which was the year *Titanic* "launched," or was slid into the water). At left we see, on May 13, 1911, 18 days before launch, workers framed by two of *Titanic*'s massive propellers. Between launch in the spring of 1911 and sailing a year later, not all went smoothly—and this had to do with the *Olympic*. On September 20, 1911, *Olympic* collided with HMS *Hawke*, and back in Belfast work was redirected to fixing a gash in the big girl's side. This ultimately delayed the maiden voyage of the *Olympic*'s sister by three weeks. Would things have been different if *Titanic* had sailed in March of 1912 rather than April? Would a different route have been chosen? Would the fateful iceberg have been in that particular place?

★

kay, statistics fans, here we go! As a prelude to our fun- and fact-filled interlude—yes, a prelude to an interlude—it is interesting to note that before *Titanic* launched, and after her sinking, the *Olympic* was for two brief periods the largest ship afloat—and was eventually altered to include much more interior space and thus become "bigger" than her sister had been. However, *Titanic*, during her time at sea, was quite deservedly celebrated as the world's biggest ship. White Star hoped that the two of them, together, would be considered the twin belles of the ball (and, when eventually joined by what was unofficially called *Gigantic*—strategically named *Britannic* after the *Titanic* went down—the *three* finest). The *Titanic* was, well . . . titanic: 882 feet, 9 inches in length; 92 feet wide; 59 feet tall above the water line; with a gross registered tonnage of 46,328. Each of three massive engines drove a propeller and was fueled by men shoveling coal into 159 coal-burning furnaces that in turn powered 29 boilers. High above, those four triumphant funnels (smokestacks, to landlubbers) were each 62 feet tall—more than 20 yards high!—so as you look at the photograph at left, you can get a sense of the ship's immensity. In that photograph, *Titanic* is sitting placidly at the fitting-out wharf of the Harland & Wolff shipyard. Between her launch in 1911 and the maiden voyage in 1912, she was kitted out with all manner of amenity and decoration. (We will detail this opulence on the pages immediately following.) Above is a contemporary photo of the dry dock at Harland & Wolff that more than a century ago housed, and nurtured, *Titanic*. Today: hallowed ground.

Regarding these and subsequent photographs: Most are from the *Titanic,* some are not—some are from the *Olympic,* designed by the same team behind the *Titanic*—but taken as a whole they paint an accurate picture of life aboard the great ship. We will distinguish in the captions. While we're on this point: Our statistics regarding the number on board on the fatal voyage—and therefore the number of dead—represent the very best estimates. Some ticket-holders may have arrived late; there may have been stowaways. We will never know, and different historians put different numbers of survivors on different lifeboats. The numbers in this book are, we hope and believe, as close as you can come. Now then: The *Olympic* and *Titanic* actually were what they were called in their day: floating hotels. Immense beyond belief at the time, they were able to offer a sense of luxury impossible on any other conveyance (the same remains true of the large luxury liners today). What the operators of dirigibles and, much later, the supersonic Concorde offered in air travel was certainly splendid. The Orient Express rail experience was extraordinary. But in 1912 a *Titanic* voyage in First Class was like sailing in the Savoy. Opposite we see the forward grand staircase on the *Olympic,* a virtual replica of the *Titanic*'s two grand staircases, which, fit for a bride, were more than 60 feet from the lower landing to the glass skylight above, decorated in 17th century William and Mary style, with carved oak railings, borders and paneling. At right, top, is the *Titanic*'s Café Parisien, which featured a French waitstaff. Center is one of 24 private suites (this one, Suite B60) located on the Bridge Deck ("B Deck," to *Titanic* cognoscenti); there were 30 more on the Shelter Deck (C Deck). Each featured up to five rooms—perhaps two bedrooms, a drawing room, a wardrobe room, etc.—and were done up in different styles (three different Kings Louis, XIV, XV or XVI, or Queen Anne, Empire, Italian Renaissance, Modern and Old Dutch, Adam or Georgian; take your pick. B60 was Queen Anne). The photograph beneath is of the *Olympic*'s First Class Lounge, located, like *Titanic*'s, on the Promenade Deck (A Deck), decorated in Louis XV style with intricately carved boiseries. Louis XIV's and Louis XVI's protests are acknowledged.

The *Titanic* was built to accommodate 735 First Class passengers, 674 in Second Class and 1,026 in Third Class, or steerage. ("Steerage" was classically a large dormitory in the depths of a ship. The White Star Line's Olympic-class vessels included semiprivate cabins for all Third Class passengers, and the firm hoped to eliminate the term *steerage* from its lexicon altogether. It stuck nonetheless, but again: *Titanic*'s below-decks accommodations were far better than ordinary "steerage.") As for life up above: splendid indeed. The *Olympic* and *Titanic* were the first luxury liners to feature not only Turkish baths (*Titanic*'s ornately tiled cooling room, top), two "electric baths" (essentially one-person sweatboxes) and a swimming pool (bottom, *Titanic*'s— called a "swimming bath") but also a squash racquets court. Their First Class Dining Saloons (right, *Olympic*'s) were elegant in the extreme, with such features as leaded glass windows.

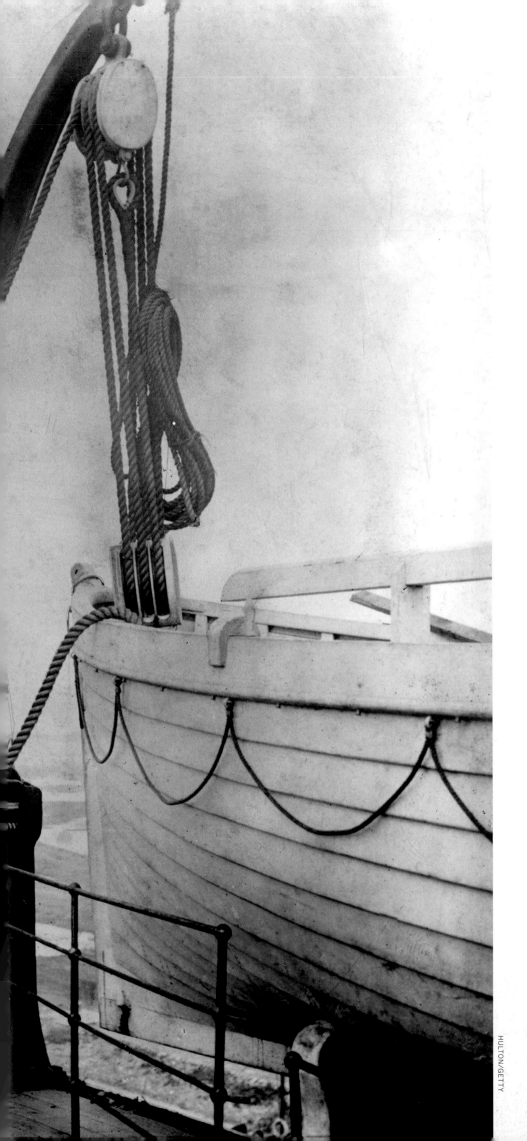

I n a ship filled with a multitude of fabulous features, a utilitarian one had been ill-planned: the supply of lifeboats. There are reasons for this, and whether these reasons are defensible was debated back in the day and is debated still. Luxury ships had grown fourfold in the first decade of the 20th century, and designers were still finding their way: What's needed? What goes where? There was no preceding disaster of a similarly huge craft to model the *Titanic*'s prospects against; *Titanic*'s catastrophe would be the precedent disaster for all that followed. It is said that some higher-ups at the Harland & Wolff shipyard wanted as many as 64 lifeboats barnacled to their vessel, though rules of the British Board of Trade, regulator of maritime safety, required only 16 for plus-size ships of more than 10,000 tons: lifeboats enough for a few more than a thousand passengers. A dissenting argument at Harland & Wolff held that high-paying passengers on the Promenade Deck wanted to enjoy the open air, and that a ship thoroughly outfitted with lifeboats would be unappealing and even forbidding, in the sense of foreboding. Ultimately, *Titanic* carried 20 lifeboats: 16 wooden and four collapsible. Anyone doing the math would have quickly concluded that in an ultimate catastrophe, these craft could be used by fewer than half of the passengers and crew aboard.

The launched *Titanic* (and, no, there was no Champagne bottle, despite what you've seen in movies) did a bit of a debut stroll in the Irish Sea and the English Channel before heading for New York City. From the harbor in Belfast, she crossed to Southampton, England, where on the 10th of April hundreds boarded (left), some having taken that morning's "Titanic Special" from Waterloo Station in London (below). The ship then proceeded from Southampton to Cherbourg, France, to pick up additional passengers—but not without ominous incident. When *Titanic* moved out of port in Southampton, an enormous displacement of water caused the steamer *New York* to break its moorings and be sucked into the huge boat's wake. It was only quick action by the *Titanic*'s attendant tugboats, including the *Hector* and *Neptune* (bottom), that kept things on schedule. Had there been a more consequential crash, and had *Titanic* been sidelined, might greater disaster have been averted?

Titanic's last port of call after Cherbourg—where she added 275 passengers including, among 142 First Class customers, the American businessman John Jacob Astor IV—was Queenstown, back in Ireland. Here it arrived at 11:30 a.m. on April 11, and took on 120 people of a different societal stripe than those who had boarded in France: none in First Class and seven in Second, but 113 in steerage. Opposite we see *Titanic*-bound passengers on a White Star ferry in Queenstown, and above we see the queue waiting to board such ferries to the outer anchorage at Roches Point where the *Titanic* is moored. Queenstown is interesting, and so is Astor. While Belfast is in the north of Ireland, Queenstown, now named Cobh, is in the far south, a sheltered seaport town in County Cork. Oddly enough, the *Titanic*'s is not Queenstown's most famous departure. Just before Christmas in 1891, the three Moore children, among others, sailed forth from this harbor for America, and on January 1, Annie Moore, who turned 15 years old that very day, became the first person registered through the new Ellis Island immigration station in New York harbor. Today, there are statues of Annie Moore in Cobh and on Ellis Island. Why was Cobh called Queenstown when Annie and, later, the *Titanic* sailed? Well, historically it had been called "the Cove of Cork," but after England's Queen Victoria visited, it was renamed in her honor in 1849. In 1922, once the Irish Free State had won its independence from Great Britain, the town was renamed, simply and with alacrity, Cobh—an Irish spelling of *cove*. As for Astor: Born in 1864 in Rhinebeck, New York, he was the great-grandson of his namesake, who built one of America's greatest-ever fortunes. John IV was in fact the wealthiest person to board the *Titanic*. He had divorced his first wife—a scandal in 1909—and in 1911, at age 47, had married 18-year-old Madeleine Talmage Force at Beechwood, the Astors' ridiculously extravagant house in Newport, Rhode Island. Fleeing the furor that their union caused in social circles back home, the Astors enjoyed an extended honeymoon in Europe and Egypt. Along the way they met, among others, the American socialite and philanthropist Margaret Brown—who would also wind up homeward bound on *Titanic*'s maiden voyage, and is remembered today as the "Unsinkable Molly Brown." The Astors and Brown struck up a friendship, but suffice it to say for now: The pregnant Madeleine and Molly would survive the *Titanic*'s sinking, and Mr. Astor would not. We will learn more about all three, as well as yet another John Jacob Astor (John IV and Madeleine's child), in our chapter "The Victims, the Survivors," beginning on page 100.

In these pictures, the bustle in Queenstown on the day a great ship sails. The "RMS" that announces the name *Titanic* stands for Royal Mail Steamer, and at left we see ponderous piles of correspondence being loaded on board a ferry in Queenstown, which will transport these bags out to a liner anchored in Deepwater Quay. Below, passengers' trunks are similarly conveyed between tender and ship. Opposite is seen a spry fellow who's been plying his wares. At the time, "traders" were vendors who licitly or illicitly boarded luxury liners and sold their goods to rich passengers; Irish lace was a hot item in Queenstown, and it is lore that John Astor had bought fine specimens before the *Titanic* weighed anchor. Safe passage for a trader could be bought by greasing the palm of a ship's officer. But then there were the "illegal traders" who simply wormed their way aboard, and sometimes were forced to escape over the side to their conspiratorial "bumboats" if they were discovered. This man is exiting, quickly, stage left, from a steamer other than the *Titanic*, in the same week that *Titanic,* too, sailed from Queenstown.

★

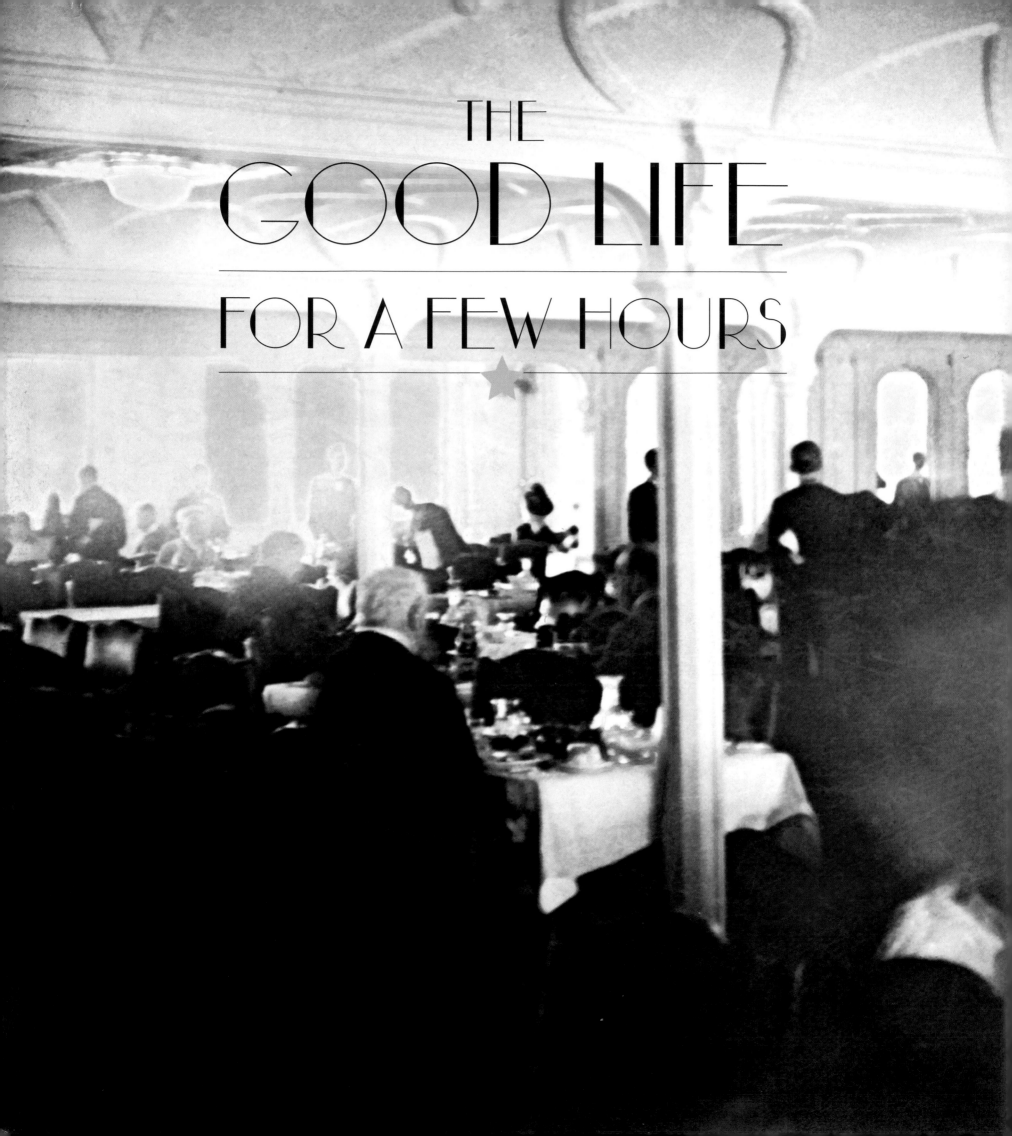

THE GOOD LIFE
FOR A FEW HOURS

Splendid doesn't begin to describe *Titanic*. The ship was splendiferous in the extreme, top to bottom, stem to stern. She needed to be; that was her charge from inception. The Cunard line of luxury cruisers already boasted the sister ships *Lusitania* (which would be torpedoed and sunk by a German U-boat in 1915) and *Mauretania,* and for the White Star Line to reasonably compete, nothing but the very best would do. It was intended that these new siblings, *Titanic, Olympic* and *Gigantic* (eventually named *Britannic*), would be nothing but the very best—the biggest and most lavishly opulent vessels ever to ply the seven seas.

The Right and Honourable Alexander Montgomery Carlisle was, early on in the White Star project, draftsman and general manager of the Harland & Wolff shipyard in Belfast, working hand-in-glove with architect Thomas Andrews on the big boats, and overseeing the decorative touches and general amenities.

Nearly as long as three football fields, as we have said, *Titanic* was showy every foot of the way. Take the fourth funnel, or smokestack: It had been added simply to make the ship look more impressive; only the other three funnels were functional (the fourth did provide a bit of ventilation). Although *Titanic* did not carry this many on her maiden and only voyage, the ship was capable of accommodating 3,547 people—

a full town of passengers and crew. The First Class Dining Saloon was worthy of the Ritz, and the swimming bath, gymnasium, squash racquets court and Turkish baths were worthy of the Downtown Athletic Club. The Café Parisien kept First Class passengers happy— or as happy as they could be after having paid a tariff of up to nearly $61,000 (in today's dollars) for a one-way transatlantic passage. (Nearly a century later, passage on the now-sidelined supersonic Concorde airplane still wouldn't cost a tenth as much.)

For four days, then, all was extravagant oceangoing bliss. Champagne glasses were clinked in celebration above deck, while down below, dances were danced by the commoners and crew in a festive whirligig, and Leonardo DiCaprio and Kate Winslet canoodled in the corner. All were having the time of their lives.

There is a term: *while it lasted.*

Titanic was everything she had been meant to be, and everything she symbolized . . .

While it lasted.

On the previous pages: Dining in style on the *Titanic*. Opposite: From high above, ship's captain, Edward John Smith (also seen in the portrait on this page) peers down at the tender. This final surviving photo of Captain Smith was made by Frank Browne, of whom we will learn more very shortly. As for Smith: He had joined the White Star Line as a young man in 1880, and by the time the *Titanic* sailed he was one of the world's most experienced sea captains—though he had suffered through more than a couple of maritime accidents when commanding the *Olympic*.

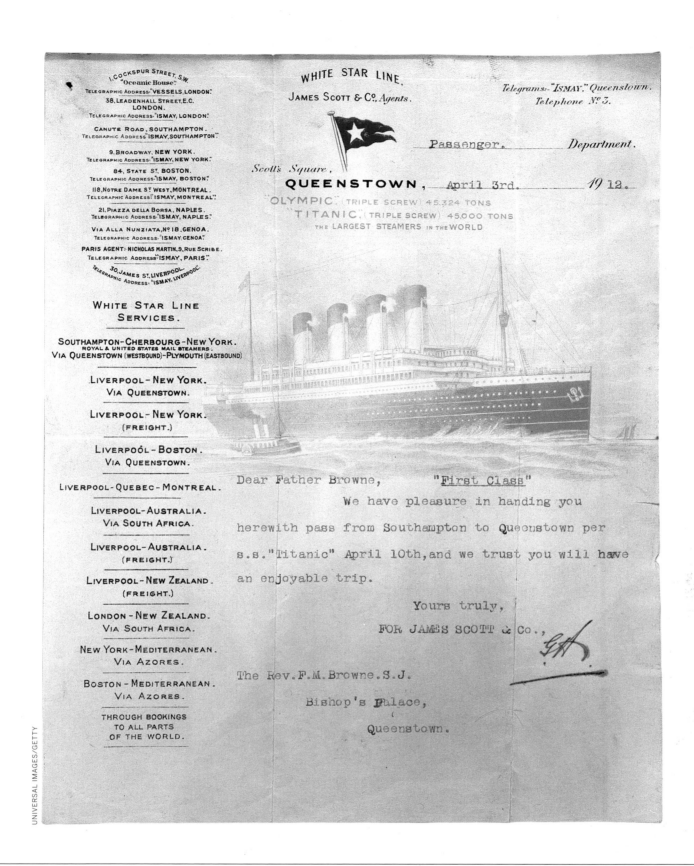

The photographic record of life on the *Titanic* is remarkably rich because of the work of one person, the Irishman Frank Browne, who took several of the pictures we have already seen and many of the ones included in this chapter. While he was a theology student in Dublin, his uncle Robert gave him a present: passage on the *Titanic*'s first legs, from Southampton to Cherbourg to Queenstown. A photographer with a brilliant eye, Browne's chronicle began with the "Titanic Special" train at Waterloo Station and continued to that final surviving image of Captain Smith peering down. He was befriended on board by a millionaire who offered to pay his passage onward from Ireland to America, but Browne's Jesuit superior put the kibosh on that via a stern cable to Queenstown: GET OFF THAT SHIP. Browne obeyed, and disembarked with a photographic record that would make his name. He became a priest in 1915, and if the shots from the *Titanic* will always be Father Browne's most famous, they were hardly his last, nor his most dramatic. In World War I, Browne was a member of the Irish Guards and documented action on the Western Front and then in postwar Germany for his regiment. Browne himself was wounded five times and was later awarded the Military Cross and Bar. After his death in 1960, his vast archive of negatives spent a quarter century resting in a large metal trunk in Dublin before it was discovered by another priest. At that point, the *Titanic* came back to life.

That a photograph of *Titanic* crewmen sporting life jackets in early 1912 would take on ominous overtones in the aftermath of the *Titanic*'s voyage could never have been foreseen. In point of fact, there were enough such jackets for all passengers and crew, and most people were wearing them when the ship sank. For this reason, relatively few people actually went down with the *Titanic,* and hundreds of floating bodies were pulled from the 31-degree water in the week following the catastrophe. Opposite, top: Passengers from steerage drink in the salt air on the *Titanic*'s Poop Deck, the closest thing to a promenade area for those in Third Class. Bottom: A purveyor of Irish lace—a legal trader—with a Captain Smith look-alike (not him; a different gent with a sporty hat).

★

In this Father Browne photograph, six-year-old Robert Douglas Spedden plays with his top as his father, Frederic, looks on. The Speddens were a very wealthy family from Tuxedo Park, New York, who were returning from one of their European Grand Tours; they had boarded *Titanic* in Cherbourg along with Mrs. Spedden's maid (one of 20 maids in First Class; there were also eight manservants) and young Douglas's nanny/nurse, Elizabeth Burns, whom Douglas called "Muddie Boons." Before departing New York a half year earlier, Douglas had been presented by an aunt with a white Steiff teddy bear, which was his constant companion. Later, after the Speddens had survived the sinking (Mr. Spedden and several other men were allowed to board Lifeboat 3 when it was about to depart unfilled), Daisy Spedden wrote a children's book, *Polar: The Titanic Bear*, as a gift for her son—a book that is still in print today. In this photo, Douglas stands in for all the children aboard the *Titanic*, whose experiences, like their parents', varied. For kids like Douglas in First Class, the world was their oyster: toys galore, that big Promenade Deck open to them, an unofficial play area in one of the two Verandah Cafés, the gymnasium available to them from one to three in the afternoon. Eleven-year-old Eileen Lenox-Conyngham, who wasn't part of the attempted passage to New York but had traveled on the *Titanic* from England to France, later recalled, "I remember vaguely the enormous dining room. Of course, it was very exciting for us because in those days children led a very nursery life, we didn't have our meals with our parents; we had them in the school or nursery. And it was generally very plain food, I suppose, like milk pudding and rather dull things like that, so it was very exciting to have this elaborate food." The food and opportunities for play were less elaborate for the children in Second Class—the gym and swimming pool were off-limits, for example—and less still for the many immigrant children in steerage. There were nearly 200 young people on the ship, and more than half of them would perish at sea, a disproportionate number being from Third Class. Thinking of this, one might quickly reflect on the good fortune of privileged Douglas Spedden, our top-spinner: He survived, as did not only his mother but also his father. Yet life, as the *Titanic* story proved to all, can turn suddenly cruel. Three years later the boy was killed in a car accident while the family was vacationing in Maine, becoming one of the very first automobile fatalities in the history of that state. On the pages immediately following: A photograph taken on the Boat Deck, another area off-limits to Third Class.

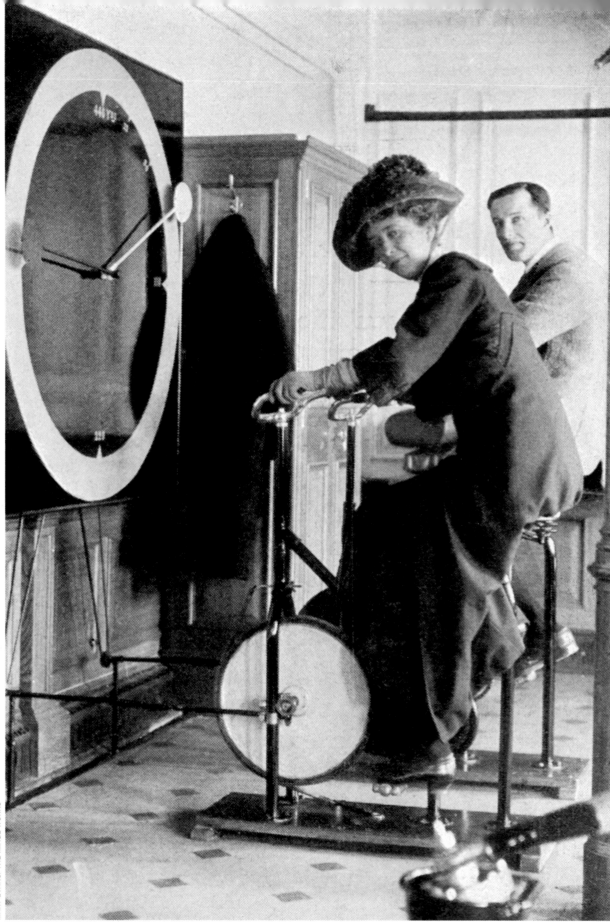

The gymnasium on the starboard side of the Boat Deck was fitted out with state-of-the-art equipment from Wiesbaden, Germany, including stationary cycles and rowing machines, two electric horses and an electric camel. The gymnasium steward was a vigorous, mustachioed Scotsman, Thomas W. McCawley, who demonstrates the equipment at left. He said as the ship was going down that he would not wear a life jacket as it would hinder his swimming. He of course perished.

I f there was a room that exemplified the idea of a floating palace quite as well as the grand staircases did, it was probably the Reading and Writing Room. Visit it here, in this Frank Browne photograph: luscious, soft white paneling, elegant furniture, a bay window on the outboard wall and luxurious window treatments throughout, a fireplace aft. This picture could have been taken in an English country house. And if it had been, Browne probably would have found a woman there, for the room was intended as a place for contemplation, to take a cup of tea or coffee, for quiet conversation—and segregation. A "reading room" in the Edwardian Era was meant for "the ladies," and here on board they gathered in the afternoon, or after dinner while the men enjoyed brandy and cigars in the Smoking Room. Conversation among the men undoubtedly included griping about how the ship wasn't proceeding fast enough through the ice field, while the women were likely engaged in more sensible discourse.

Crucial inner workings: the only photo of the *Titanic*'s radio room, known as the Marconi Operating Room, and a boiler room from another steamer. Jack "Sparks" Phillips ran the Marconi Room, assisted by Harold Bride (above), and both men stayed at their posts until minutes before the ship sank, although they already had been relieved of their duties by Captain Smith. (Phillips died; Bride survived.) As for the boiler room, a so-called Black Gang similar to this one consisted, on the *Titanic*, of 175 firemen (stokers) plus 73 trimmers, whose job was to move the coal from bunker to boiler, and whose toil yielded a top oceangoing speed of 23 knots, or 26.46 miles per hour.

★

As we have seen, *Titanic* was a legend even before she launched. In this chapter we seek to apprehend the immensity of that legend—before and after the tragedy, a legend that only continues to grow today as audiences stream to IMAX theaters to ingest or reingest the spectacle, as imagined by James Cameron, in 3-D

Back in 1912, everyone, everywhere knew the ship named *Titanic* was coming—the Astors in New York's society circles knew it, and those who read the tabloids of Fleet Street knew it. The White Star enterprise made certain of this, heralding *Titanic* as the be-all and end-all of human transport and saturnalian luxury (read: excess).

As is so often the case, lurking in the buildup was the comedown. Since the Greeks—since Homer—the greatest dramas have included adversity, comeuppance, even doom. The story of the *Titanic*, a cautionary fable for the postindustrial age, was Homeric and Shakespearean, both. It involved a state-of-the-art man-made machine and an iceberg: nature's product, perhaps 10,000 or more years old. Hubris was ascribed, if not always deservedly. (Perhaps the White Star PR folks were culpable, perhaps Captain Smith was not.)

The printed artifacts in this chapter are redolent of the era and bear witness to *Titanic*'s fame and stature as a cultural icon both before she sailed and after she sank. Note that the poster advertises a return voyage from New York City back to Europe, a trip that would, of course, never be made. It was unthinkable to White Star that their new queen was anything but unsinkable. Opposite: Superstars can sell soap.

WHITE STAR LINE

ROYAL & STEAMERS
UNITED STATES MAIL

FIRST SAILING OF THE LATEST ADDITION TO THE WHITE STAR FLEET

The Queen of the Ocean

TITANIC

LENGTH 882½ FT.   OVER 45,000 TONS TRIPLE-SCREWS   BEAM 92½ FT.

This, the Latest, Largest and Finest Steamer Afloat, will sail from
WHITE STAR LINE, PIER 59 (North River), NEW YORK

Saturday, April 20th At 12 Noon

THIRD CLASS FOUR BERTH ROOM
Spacious Dining Saloons
Smoking Room
Ladies' Reading Room
Covered Promenade

All passengers berthed in closed rooms containing 2, 4, or 6 berths, a large number equipped with washstands, etc.

THIRD CLASS DINING SALOON

Reservations of Berths may be made direct with this Office or through any of our accredited agents

THIRD CLASS RATES ARE:

To PLYMOUTH, SOUTHAMPTON, LONDON, LIVERPOOL and GLASGOW,	$36.25
To GOTHENBURG, MALMÖ, CHRISTIANIA, COPENHAGEN, ESBJERG, Etc.	41.50
To STOCKHOLM, ÅBO, HANGÖ, HELSINGFORS	44.50
To HAMBURG, BREMEN, ANTWERP, AMSTERDAM, ROTTERDAM, HAVRE, CHERBOURG	45.00

TURIN, $48.   NAPLES, $52.50.   PIRAEUS, $55.   BEYROUTH, $61., Etc., Etc.

DO NOT DELAY: Secure your tickets through the local Agents or direct from
WHITE STAR LINE, 9 Broadway, New York

TICKETS FOR SALE HERE

The headline writers went nuts on the *Titanic* in a way they rarely had. Consider: 1,500 or so people died that night. When the Mississippi paddlewheeler the SS *Sultana* exploded and burned in 1865, 1,800 people died: the worst maritime disaster in U.S. history.

The *Sultana* does not live on in our imagination, though it was, after all, an American vessel. The *Titanic*, as the typescript on these next several pages indicates, was different.

Why? Because White Star wrote the rules. The *Titanic* was designed to flaunt any norms of decency—Caligula would have booked passage—and even to defy God. "This ship is virtually unsinkable," wrote a trade journal after the White Star folks whispered in its ear. The builders, owners and first passengers nodded in assent. God looked on.

Of the original Seven Wonders of the World, only the Great Pyramid remains standing today. In 1937 the zeppelin *Hindenburg* caught fire and crashed horrifically. Two Space Shuttles went down. Rome burned while Nero fiddled. The Yankees lost a three-game lead in a best-of-seven series against the Red Sox in 2004.

Homer understood: The cost of hubris is great. The headline writers of Fleet Street and those of the august *Times* across the pond understood, too. They were very happy to build the *Titanic* up. And then they were all too eager to pounce on the tragedy, mythologize it and make it something that, a hundred years later, haunts us still.

For months there had been nothing but excitement among the Irish locals who had secured tickets to watch the 1911 launch in Belfast—and certainly among the international upper crust who had secured First Class accommodations on the next year's maiden voyage (two tickets, opposite, top). A footnote: At the launch there was no formal "christening"; White Star never went that way with its ships. Elsewhere on these pages you can read the happy prose of the passengers on that inaugural journey of the great vessel, telling the folks back home how lucky they considered themselves.

CLOCKWISE FROM FAR LEFT: MARY EVANS/THE IMAGE WORKS; SPINK SMYTHE/AP; COURTESY HOSANO FAMILY; PA/AP; GRANGER; CHRIS HONDROS/NEWSMAKERS/GETTY; MARY EVANS/EVERETT

On board R·M·S·"TITANIC".

10 / 4   1912

Dear Mr Jury,

Thanks for your letter . I just had an hours roaming about on this wonderful boat together with Paul.

TUCK'S POST CARD

POSTKARTE

(FOR ADDRESS ONLY.)

By Appointment

CELEBRATED "OILETTE" Postcard

Raphael Tuck & Sons ART PUBLISHERS TO THEIR MAJESTIES THE KING & QUEEN.

T.S.S. "Titanic" Triple-screw steamer "Titanic," launched at the White Star steamer "Titanic," one of the largest vessels afloat, belongs to the White Star Line. It is a wonderful achievement of Belfast, one of British shipyards. At present time, it is near completion and is expected to be ready for her service between Southampton and New York.

P.S. Please don't bother to send me these till you know where you are.

Dear Mother

arrived at South Hampton safe. The Titanic is a splendid boat + you hardly know you are moving. Will write more fully later. Your loving son

Mrs. Thomas Mudd.
The Street
Huntingfield
Halesworth
Suffolk
England.

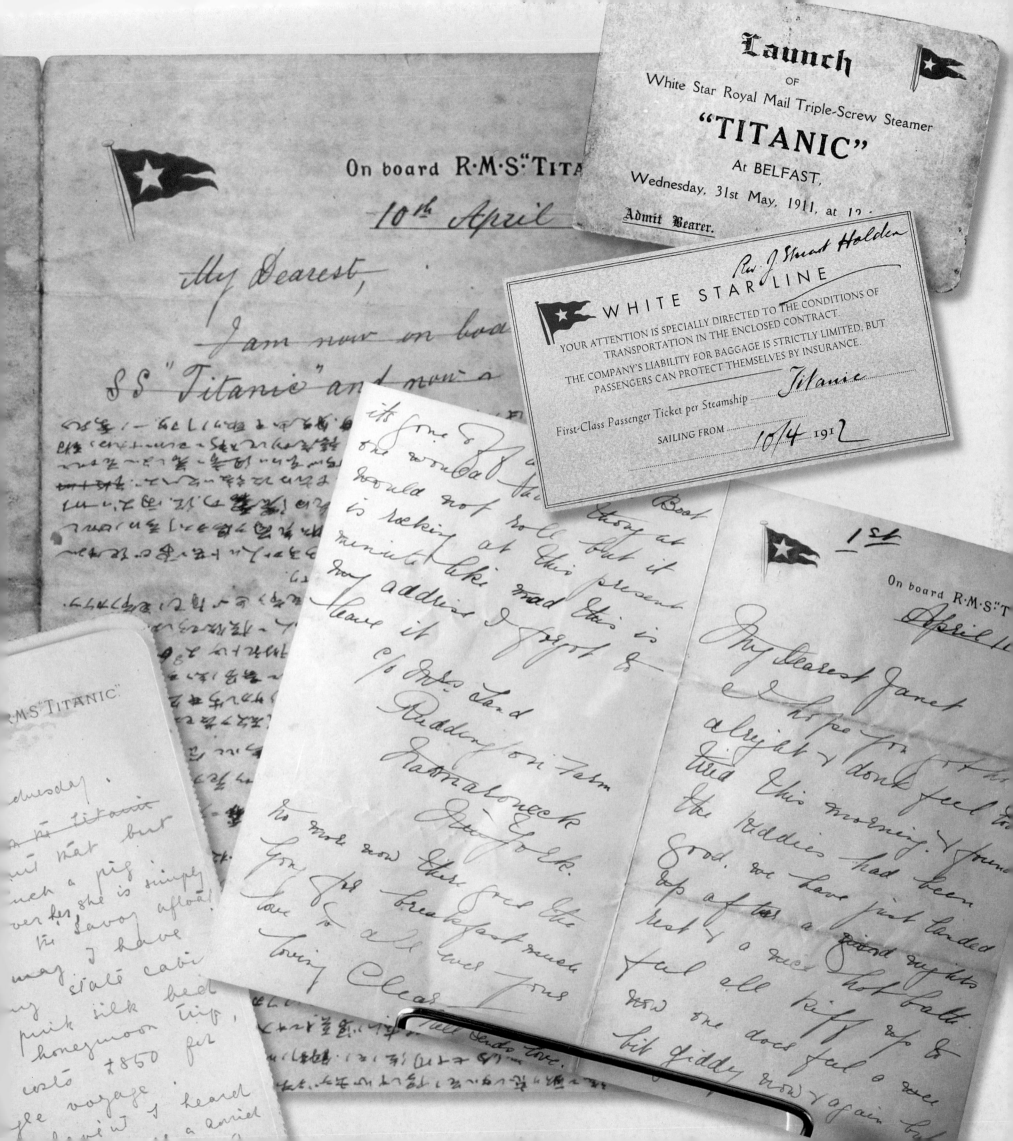

FIRST CLASS PASSENGER LIST

PER

ROYAL AND U.S. MAIL

S.S. "Titanic,"

FROM SOUTHAMPTON AND CHERBOURG

TO NEW YORK

(Via QUEENSTOWN).

Wednesday, 10th April, 1912.

Captain, E. J. Smith, R.D. (Commr. R.N.R.)

Surgeon, W. F. N. O'Loughlin.
Asst. Surgeon, J. E. Simpson.

Pursers { H. W. McElroy
R. L. Barker.

Chief Steward, A. Latimer.

Allen, Miss Elizabeth
Walton

Allison, Mr. H. J.

Allison, Mrs. H. J.
and Maid

Allison, Miss

Allison, Master
and Nurse

Anderson, Mr. Harry

Andrews, Miss Cornelia I.

Andrews, Mr. Thomas

Appleton, Mrs. E. D.

Artagaveytia, Mr. Ramon

Astor, Colonel J. J.
and Manservant

Astor, Mrs. J. J.
and Maid

Aubert, Mrs. N.
and Maid

Those on the passenger list on this page were almost exclusively among high society's crème de la crème: You just wouldn't drop that kind of money to get from here to there unless you possessed money to burn and great savoir faire. At times many of these First Class passengers surely behaved with noblesse oblige toward the ship's crew (which in fact was under instructions to make itself as invisible as possible), as well as whatever Second and Third Class less-fortunate confreres or consoeurs they might chance upon. At dinner hour, when ship bugler Peter W. Fletcher marched deck to deck sounding the White Star Line's traditional mess call, "The Roast Beef of Old England," those in First Class would head to the Reception Room for an aperitif before proceeding on to the Dining Saloon on D Deck. *Crèmes, confreres, aperitifs:* all these French phrases! Well, English roast beef might be heralded in song, but it simply wouldn't suffice in First Class, where there was fine French cuisine and the finest French wine as well. Please don't feel too bad for those in steerage: Only recently, Third Class passengers had been forced to bring their own food on such immigrant journeys, and what the *Titanic* offered them was by and large better than what they had eaten at home only yesterday. A last, poignant note: The menu dated April 14 was for luncheon on the very last day.

R.M.S. "TIT[ANIC]

APRIL 10, [1912]

HORS D'ŒUVRE VARIÈS

CONSOMMÉ RÉJANE   CRÈME REINE M[ARY]

TURBOT, SAUCE HOMARD

WHITEBAIT

MUTTON CUTLETS & GREEN PEAS

SUPRÊME OF CHICKEN À LA STANLEY

SIRLION OF BEEF, CHÂTEAU POTATOE[S]

ROAST DUCKLING, APPLE SAUCE

FILLET OF VEAL & BRAISED HA[M]

CAULIFLOWER

BOILED RICE

BOVIN & BOILED NEW PO[TATOES]

PLOVER ON TOAST &

SALAD

PUDDING SANS [SOUCI]

CHARLOTTE

GRANV[ILLE]

FRENCH ICE[S]

R.M.S. "TITANIC"

LUNCHEON.

APRIL 14, 1912.

CONSOMMÉ FERMIER

FILLETS OF BRILL   COCKIE LEEKIE

EGG À L'ARGENTEUIL

CHICKEN À LA MARYLAND

CORNED BEEF, VEGETABLES, DUMPLINGS

FROM THE GRILL.

GRILLED MUTTON CHOPS

MASHED, FRIED & BAKED JACKET POTATOES

CUSTARD PUDDING   PASTRY

BUFFET.

APPLE MERINGUE   POTTED SHRIMPS

SALMON MAYONNAISE   SOUSED HERRINGS

NORWEGIAN ANCHOVIES   PLAIN & SMOKED SARDINES

ROUND OF SPICED BEEF

VEAL & HAM PIE

VIRGINIA & CUMBERLAND HAM

BOLOGNA SAUSAGE   GALANTINE OF CHICKEN

CORNED OX TONGUE

LETTUCE   BEETROOT   TOMATOES

CHEESE.

CHESHIRE, STILTON, GORGONZO[LA]

CAMEMBERT, ROQUEFO[RT]

CH[EDDAR]

Iced draught Munich La[ger]

WHITE STAR LINE.

R.M.S. "TITANIC."

APRIL 12, 1912.

THIRD CLASS.

BREAKFAST.

OATMEAL PORRIDGE & MILK

SMOKED HERRINGS, JACKET POTATOES

TRIPE & ONIONS

FRESH BREAD & BUTTER

MARMALADE   SWEDISH BREAD

TEA   COFFEE

DINNER.

PEA SOUP

FRESH BREAD   CABIN BISCUITS

LING FISH, EGG SAUCE

HOT POT   POTATOES

STEWED APPLES & RICE

TEA.

PICKED COD

CURRY & RICE

FRESH BREAD & BUTTER

SWEDISH BREAD

JAM

TEA

SUPPER.

GRUEL

CABIN BISCUITS   CHEESE

Any complaint respecting the Food supplied, want of attention or incivility, should be at once reported to the Purser or Chief Steward. For purposes of identification, each Steward wears a numbered badge on the arm.

Titanic's wireless equipment was cutting edge—it could reach out 250 miles or more during the day and up to 2,000 miles at night—and its operators, Jack Phillips and Harold Bride (who is seen on page 44), were dedicated and skilled. This combination might have led to a vastly different outcome had the radiomen's talents extended to a fluency in German. At top left is the English version of a transmission sent from the German ship *Amerika* to the *Titanic* warning of icebergs in the area—but the original transmission was never translated. The other transmissions on this page are just as eerie, indicating a professional calm over three hours as the catastrophe unfolded. At 1:37 a.m., *Baltic* told *Titanic*: "We are rushing to you." Three minutes later *Olympic* assured: "Am lighting up all possible boilers as fast as can." In the event, *Carpathia* would get there first—but still too late. As the *Titanic* lost all power and the Marconi Room switched to its battery-powered transmitter, this last message went out sometime after 2:15: "We are sinking fast. Passengers are being put into boats." At 2:20, the *Virginian* asked the *Olympic*: "Have you heard anything about RMS *Titanic*." The reply: "No. Keeping strict watch, but hear nothing more from RMS *Titanic*. No reply from her."

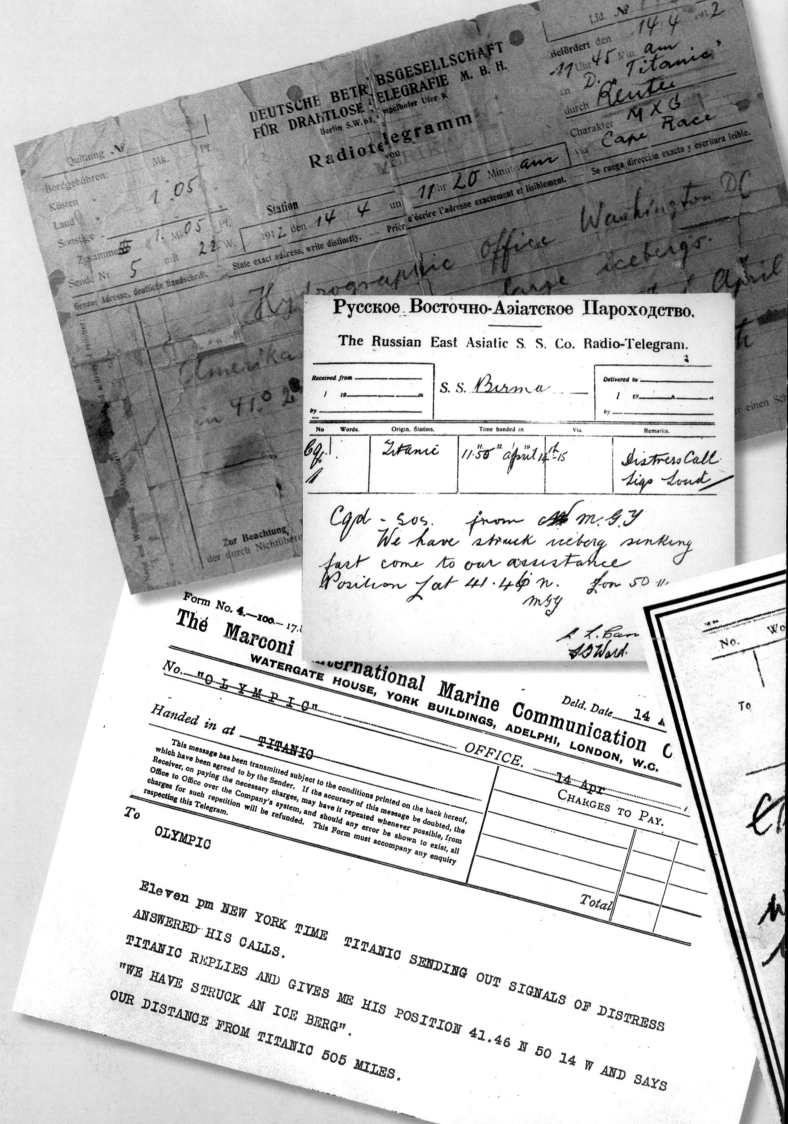

The Marconi International Marine Communication

WATERGATE HOUSE, YORK BUILDINGS, ADELPHI, LONDON, W

Sent date

No. 9126 **"CARPATHIA"** OFFICE

Prefix — Code — Words 6

Office of Origin "CARPATHIA"

Service Instructions :

Marconi C...
Other Li...
Delivery...
To...
Office...

READ THE CONDITIONS PRINTED ON THE BACK OF

To : Harry W. Dodge

Pacific Hardware and Stee
San Francisco

All Safe. Notify
Vida

CONINGHAM BROS., Printers, etc., Limehouse, E.

The Marconi International Marine Communication Company, Ltd.

WATERGATE HOUSE, YORK BUILDINGS, ADELPHI, LONDON, W.C.

Sent date 1912

No. 1021 of Carpathia

Prefix of Carpathia OFFICE

Office of Origin — Code — Words 3 R Apl

Service Instructions :

CHARGES TO PAY.
Marconi Charge ...
Other Line Charge ...
Delivery Charge ...
Total

To : BEIRNES Beirnes

State St West Orange

No. — Words — Origin. Station. — Time handed in. — Vis. — Remarks.

— H. M. — 19—

To

CQ mGY
boats

Women and Children in
cannot last much longer
mGY

Origin. Station: — Time handed in.

— H — M — 19—

Titanic

SOS SOS CQD CQD — m

are sinking fast pa
ng put into boats

Signal Station at Cape Race cables:-

...5 p.m. Titanic reports by wireless struck iceberg and calls
for immediate assistance at 11 p.m. she reported sinking by head
women being put off in boats gave position as 41.46 N. 50.14 W.
Baltic Olympic and Virginian all making towards scene disaster latter
was last to hear Titanic signals at 12-27 a.m. reported them then
blurred and ending abruptly believed Virginian will be first ship
to reach .

REPORT   April 15, 1-27 p.m.

LLOYD'S LIST.
CASUALTY REPORT Apr.15, 2-34 p.m.

TITANIC (s)

...ge.Tel. Co's telegram dated New York Apr.15 states:-
...less message received at Halifax at 4-30 this morning stated
...est of the passengers from the TITANIC had been put in the life-
...ats and that the sea was calm:

...an Exchange Tel. Co's telegram dated New York Apr.15 states:-
The White Star officials here state that the Virginian is standing
by the TITANIC and that there is no danger of loss of life.

In the aftermath of the tragedy, few of the many, many stories that arrived with the survivors captivated the public as much as the ones about the music: the music that continued to be heard as the ship foundered, the music of the band that heroically played on. In the nature of these things, various episodes have perhaps grown beyond fact into legend. What is known for sure: Bandleader Wallace Hartley did gather his men and begin to play, moving the eight-piece orchestra out to the Boat Deck after midnight when all of the activity moved outdoors. And Hartley and his colleagues did indeed play until 2 a.m., when the deck began to tilt at a violent angle; many survivors confirm this. All eight men perished. What else do we know? Well, in movie scores like the one for James Cameron's film, the reputation of composer Francis Popy (above) has been rightly resurrected since his Belle Epoque waltzes surely were popular with the *Titanic*'s passengers and would have buoyed them as the crisis deepened. Was the last song really the all-too-perfect "Nearer My God to Thee"? At least one survivor reportedly said so in New York and the newspapers ran with it (the commemorative score shown at right features Captain Smith's portrait, not Hartley's). But this could have been a borrowed finale: The passengers and crew of the SS *Valencia* had indeed sung the 18th century hymn as their ship went down off Canada in 1906, and this earlier incident was widely known. Then, too, some survivors thought "Song d'Automne" was the last they could hear as their *Titanic* lifeboats drifted away. The answer is one that will never be resolved, but what *is* known: At Hartley's funeral in the Lancashire town of Colne, in England—attended by 30,000—services ended with "Nearer My God to Thee."

ARCHE DE PARIS

SIBRE   FRANCIS POPY

Dès le ma_tin   lors_que la nuit's_ache

IC."

TONNAGE. 46,192.

ON
MAIDEN
VOYAGE,
15th APRIL. 1912.

NEARER MY GOD TO THEE!

Nearer,   my God,   to Thee,   Nearer   to   Thee;

E'en though it   be   a cross   That   raiseth   me:

cres.   tempo.   Still all my song shall be,   Nearer, my God, to Thee,   Nearer to Thee

Though like the wanderer,
The sun gone down,
Darkness comes over me,
My rest a stone,
Yet in my dreams I'd be
Nearer, my God, to Thee,
Nearer to Thee.

There let my way appear
Steps unto Heav'n,
All that Thou sendest me
In mercy given,
Angels to beckon me
Nearer, my God, to Thee,
Nearer to Thee.

Then, with my
Bright
Out of my s
Beth-e
So by my u
Nearer, my
Nea

Hymn played by Bandsmen of the S.S. "TITANIC" as
her doom, 15th April, 1912.

Funnel for auxiliary Machinery & ventilation

SPACE OCCUPIED BY RECIPROCATING & TURBINE ENGINES

WATER LINE

3 Forward Funnels carrying off Products of combustion from Main Boilers

SPACE OCCUPIED BY BOILERS

Facts—about everything from songs to the number of victims to rumors of sabotage— were elusive, as the masses demanded to know: *What happened?* Some of the same papers that were claiming that "Nearer My God to Thee" had accompanied the ship beneath the waves also said *Titanic* was being towed to Halifax. But as better reporting, followed by official inquiries, confirmed the worst, any false hope about the magnitude of the disaster faded. A London weekly, *The Sphere,* did a fair job with the terrifying moment of the stern rising above the sea (opposite); as mentioned, it would be 73 years before the wreck was found, and we learned that *Titanic* had split in two as the stern soared. At right we have an affidavit by Laura Mabel Francatelli to the British *Titanic* inquiry. She recalls the "awful rumbling" as the ship sank— "then came the screams and cries." Francatelli, 31, was secretary to Lucy Christiana (a.k.a. Lady Duff-Gordon), whom we will meet in our next chapter. Francatelli admits that she, Lucy Christiana and her husband, Sir Cosmo Duff-Gordon, had boarded one of the last lifeboats to depart; that it had contained only 12; and that there had been no thought of going back for others. Through testimony of such as hers, the *Titanic* story began to take shape and become truer.

MISS MABEL FRANCATELLI of 72 Strathbrook Road, Streatham Says:-

I am Secretary of Lady Duff Gordon and accompanied her to New York.

I was a passenger on the Titanic.

My Cabin being on "E" Deck which I believe was about 20 feet above the water line.

After the collision I stood in the corridor outside my cabin. At last the water began to make its way in so I went up to the cabin of Lady Duff Gordon who was on "A" Deck, the top.

A man came to me and put a life preserver on me assuring me it was only taking precautions and not to be alarmed.

When we got on the top deck the life-boats were being lowered on the starboard side.

I then noticed that the sea was nearer to us than during the day, and I said to Sir Cosmo Duff Gordon "We are sinking" and he said "Nonsense come away".

The men wished to put Lady Duff Gordon and myself into a life boat but we refused to leave Cosmo Gordon. Sir Cosmo then said to me "Here, Miss Franks, you must go" or words to that effect but I refused again saying I would not leave Lady Duff Gordon. Other life boats were then lowered.

As they were letting down the last life boat on our side there was a call for "Any more women" and they pulled at Lady Duff Gordon and myself, but we again refused to go, so they lowered the life boat without us. It was the last life-boat.

Everybody then seemed to rush away to the other side of the ship and left our side quite empty, but we remained there as Sir Cosmo Duff Gordon said we must wait for orders. Presently an officer started to swing out a little boat, quite an ordinary little rowing boat and ordered some stokers to man it.

There were no other women there by that time. The Officer saw us and ordered us in, and we said we would go if Sir Cosmo could come also. The officer said to Sir Cosmo "I should be pleased if you would go" We were dropped into this boat and lowered into the sea. Just as they were lowering the boat two American Gentlemen came along the deck and got in also. The Officers gave orders to us to row away from the ship.

There were seven sailors in the boat Lady Duff Gordon, myself Sir Cosmo and the two American gentlemen. Twelve in all.

The boat was not a lifeboat, but quite a small ordinary rowing boat and not too safe. It could not have lived in high waves for five minutes, in fact it was of so little use that when the Carpathia picked us up they let our boat go and did not trouble to take it aboard the Carpathia.

MABEL FRANCATE

29

B. & D. 26

General Register and Record Office of Shipping and Seamen,
Tower Hill, London, E.

CERTIFIED EXTRACT RELATING TO THE SUPPOSED DEATH OF A SEAMAN.

This is to Certify that the List of Crew, required by Section 255 of the Merchant Shipping Act, 1894, to be furnished by the Master or Owner of a lost or abandoned Ship, has been deposited in this Office in respect of the

Titanic of *Liverpool* Official Number *131428*.

The Ship is described as *lost 15th April 1912 about Lat. 41. 16 N, Long. 50. 14 W.*

and *E. Stone* Birthplace *Hants.* aged *33* is stated to have been serving on board at the time in the capacity of *Bedroom Steward* and is supposed to have been drowned.

Examined by

Office Fee *Fourpence*.

Henry to Inalan

Registrar-General of Shipping and Seamen.

Dated this *20th* day of *June*, 191*2*.

Printed by DRAKE, DRIVER & LEAVER, LTD., Rosebery Avenue, London, E.C.

I n a century, we have sorted out much. There were two bedroom stewards named E. Stone on the crew of the *Titanic*, an Edward and an Edmund, and only in recent years do their families feel they have figured out who was buried at sea, and who rests in a *Titanic* section of a graveyard in Nova Scotia. The artist's illustration of the North Atlantic opposite, published after the disaster, is fairly accurate although not to scale. The headlines on the following four pages reflect the general confusion and horror—and also imply just how big a deal was the *Titanic*, and her loss.

★

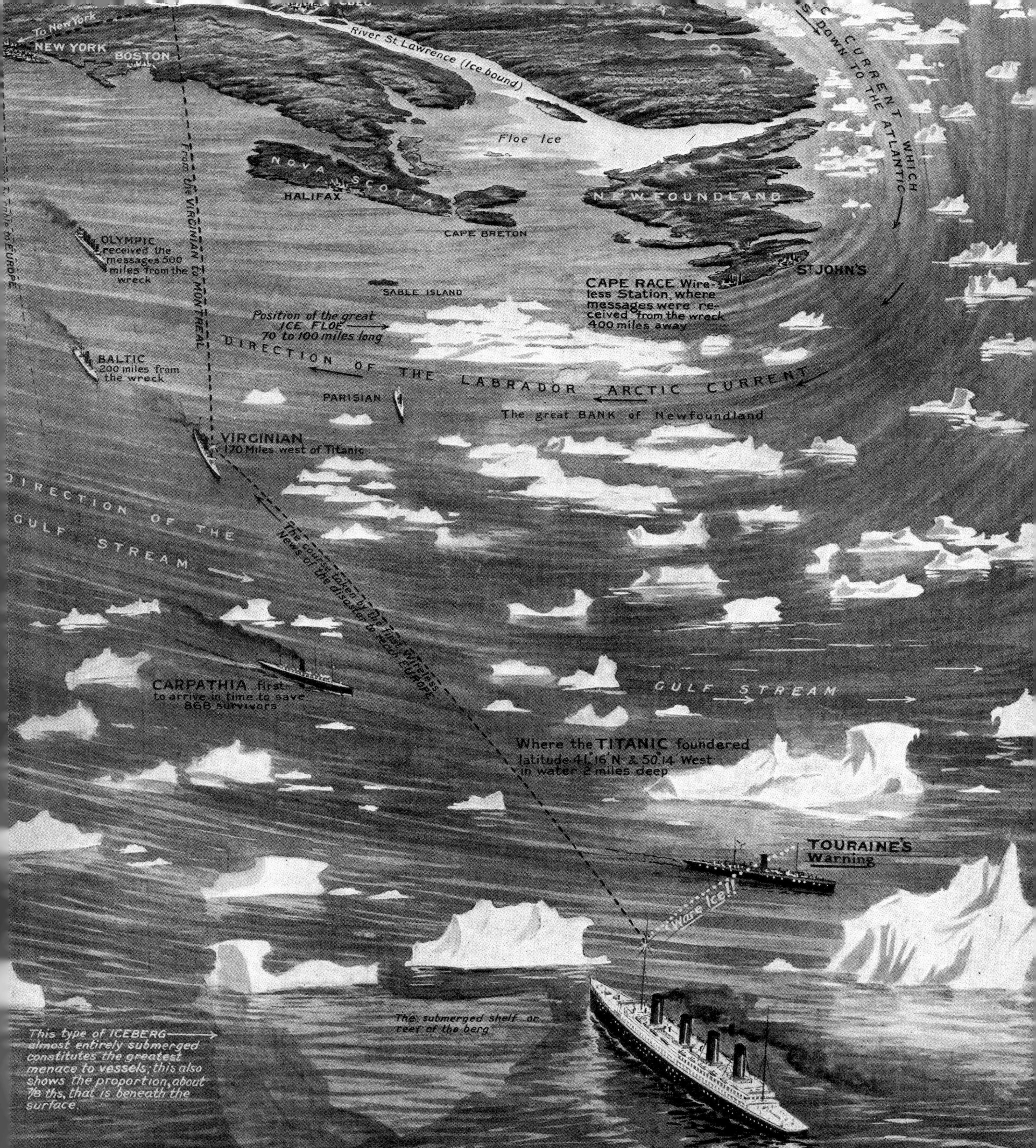
To New York
NEW YORK
BOSTON
River St. Lawrence (Ice bound)
CURRENT WHICH
DOWN TO THE ATLANTIC
Floe Ice
NOVA SCOTIA
HALIFAX
CAPE BRETON
NEWFOUNDLAND
ST JOHN'S
From the VIRGINIAN to MONTREAL
OLYMPIC received the messages 500 miles from the wreck
SABLE ISLAND
CAPE RACE Wireless Station, where messages were received from the wreck 400 miles away
Position of the great ICE FLOE 70 to 100 miles long
DIRECTION OF THE LABRADOR ARCTIC CURRENT
BALTIC 200 miles from the wreck
PARISIAN
The great BANK of Newfoundland
VIRGINIAN 170 Miles west of Titanic
DIRECTION OF THE GULF STREAM
The course taken by the First Wireless News of the disaster to reach EUROPE
CARPATHIA first to arrive in time to save 868 survivors
GULF STREAM
Where the TITANIC foundered latitude 41°16'N & 50°14' West in water 2 miles deep
TOURAINE'S Warning
'Ware Ice!!
The submerged shelf or reef of the berg
This type of ICEBERG almost entirely submerged constitutes the greatest menace to vessels; this also shows the proportion, about 7/8 ths, that is beneath the surface.

In this pictorial diagram it was

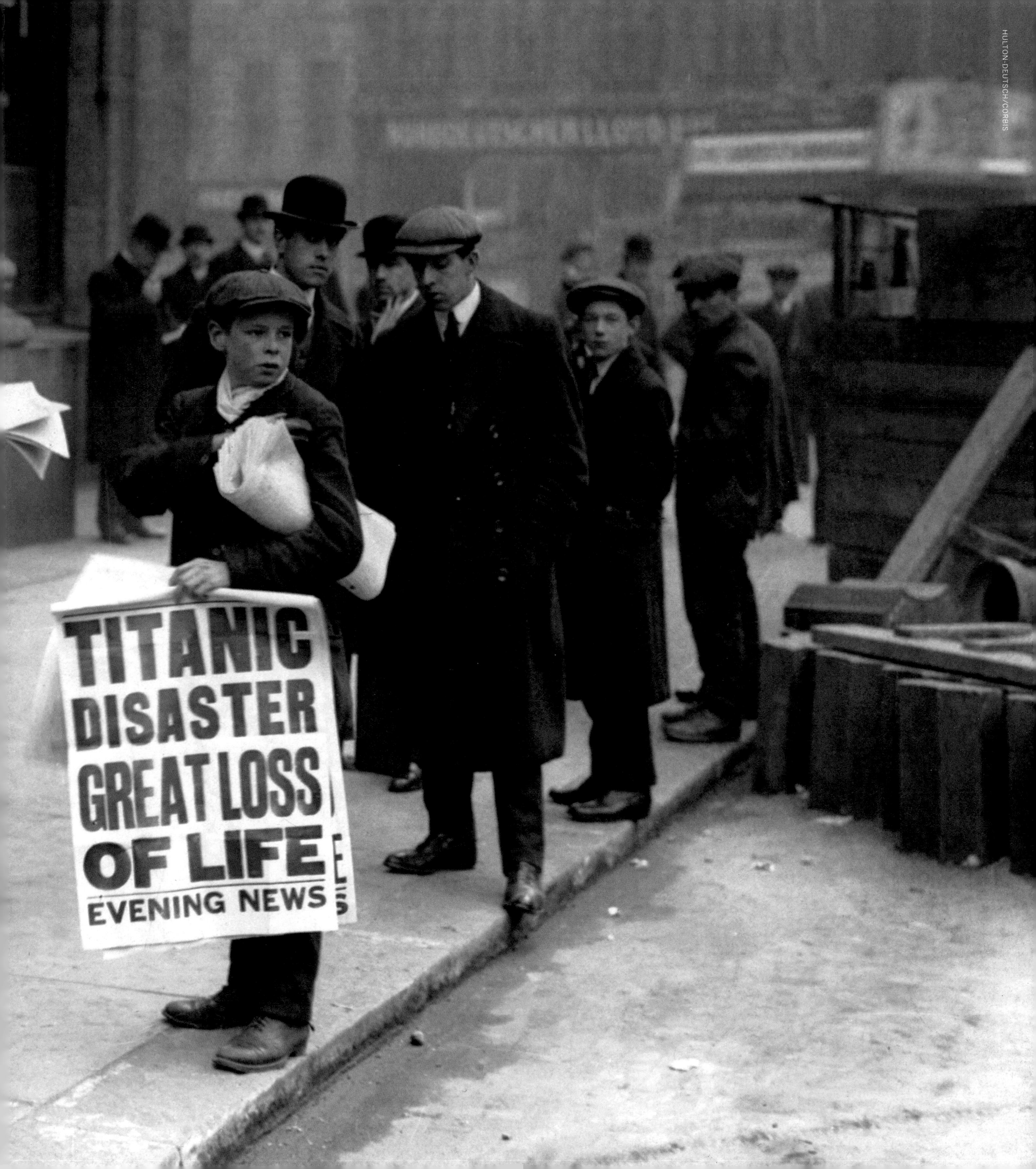

HULTON-DEUTSCH/CORBIS

THE
ICEBERG
AND
AFTERWARD

Copyright

Wain Wood S.S. Ironian

The actual event makes for a strange photographic record, particularly for a modern audience. We all have grown up with *you-are-there* images of home runs being hit, touchdowns being scored, Presidents being shot, towers falling, Brad and Angelina kissing. The camera is always present to record the critical event. *The crucial moment.*

Not so with the *Titanic*. But as it turns out, the dramatic happenings just before and after the ship went down—the diners aboard the doomed vessel, the survivors clambering aboard the *Carpathia*—are well and eloquently documented in pictures. We have an intriguing visual narrative. We see the fore story graphically, the nearly three hours before the awful denouement. And we see the desperate aftermath. We are forced, however, as if we were reading a masterly novel, to imagine the horror that overwhelmed the ship: the flooded bow turning down, plunging, the ship severing—as no one was sure it had until 1985, when the wreckage was finally found—and the stern plummeting separately, all just approximately two hours and 40 minutes after hitting the iceberg.

It's odd—certainly the term *it's funny* cannot be used—how casually the tragedy occurred and how slowly the extent of it was

On the previous two pages and then here, we see what the *Titanic* confronted—in photographs taken days before the tragedy. The iceberg on the earlier pages is believed to be the culprit berg; the words written on the picture, penned by Captain Wood of the SS *Etonian*, testify to his conviction that this, seen by him from his ship on April 12, was the one. The ice field at right was photographed even earlier, on April 4, from the deck of another ship, and at the approximate location of the eventual tragedy.

apprehended. The starboard area forward, beneath the waterline, glanced the iceberg and was breached. If architect Thomas Andrews knew right away what this might mean, others having been informed that the ship was in desperate straits—others including even Captain Smith—needed to be convinced. Which is not to say that Smith and his colleagues acted with anything other than urgency. The two hours following the initial incident were fueled with purposeful energy and, indeed, with many expressions of valor. By the time the extent of the disaster was made clear to all, there was little more to be said or done but to flee. And by then all of the lifeboats but two had been launched.

In the pages of this chapter, there are stories of what might have been and what was. Icebergs were common in the North Atlantic, and so were other big boats. The *Titanic* was in possession of Marconi technology, which proved a very good thing, but not every ship in the general vicinity was heroic enough on the frigid night to rush to the stricken ship's rescue. This was unfortunate.

Unfortunate.

That's an unfortunate word to use, even a hundred years on, when we know how many died. It is a dispassionate, uncommitted word.

Tragic.

That's the word that has most often been put to this story: the tragedy of the *Titanic*. It is apt.

A *Titanic* lifeboat approaches the rescue ship *Carpathia*. In addition to the 16 wooden lifeboats like this one, there were an additional four with collapsible, watertight canvas sides that allowed for relatively flat storage on deck. The collapsibles were 27.5 feet long by eight wide, with a depth of three feet, and could carry up to 47 people; most of the wooden boats could accomodate 65, though few left with a full complement of passengers.

On the next eight pages, the dramatic story of the *Carpathia*'s rescue mission is told. As to what these pictures represent: There were no photographs taken (and therefore none exist) of the sinking itself or of the action on deck, and so when the images you see here are elsewhere sometimes labeled "lifeboats launching with survivors," they are mislabeled. First and foremost, there would have been no daylight. These two photographs in fact depict the purposeful action on the *Carpathia* on the morning of April 15, when Captain Arthur Henry Rostron and his crew gathered the *Titanic*'s survivors, many still in shock and many suffering from frostbite or hypothermia. (The photograph opposite shows Lifeboat 12, the last to be hoisted and drained.) The *Carpathia*'s men brought on board, as well, some of the *Titanic*'s most recently deceased, those who hadn't made it through the night. No other vessel rescued anyone. Another steamship, the *Californian* (British, despite the name), was closer than the *Carpathia* (which had been 58 nautical miles away), but, after warning the *Titanic* of icebergs in the area, the *Californian* hadn't moved all night. Some later testimony maintained that men aboard the *Californian* saw the *Titanic*'s distress rockets, and even saw lights go out on the great ship, yet the *Californian*'s wireless operations remained shut down until dawn. The *Carpathia*, by contrast, received *Titanic*'s distress signal and leapt into action. Wireless operator Harold Cottam woke Captain Rostron, who ordered full steam ahead. His engineering crew turned off the heating and nonessential electricity to divert energy to more urgent matters, and, according to Rostron, coaxed the ship up to 17.5 knots, three and a half more than her top service speed. An intrepid mission zigzagging through the ice fields that might have taken five hours took barely more than three. Rostron ordered extra lookouts posted to navigate the ice, and ordered starburst flares fired to let the *Titanic* know she was coming. He asked his crew and passengers to pile up the blankets (on the following pages: *Titanic* survivors on the *Carpathia*'s Hurricane Deck after they had been supplied with wraps by women passengers aboard the rescue ship) and ordered his medical crew to ready dining rooms as hospital wards. He issued 23 orders in all, and saved the day—as much as it could ever be saved.

The *Carpathia*, having made her way
past no fewer than six potentially crip-
pling icebergs, began taking on survivors about an hour after the outermost
lifeboats of *Titanic* had first seen the rescue
ship's starburst rockets, and had adjusted
their course, rowing hard to salvation.
Ultimately, Captain Rostron and crew would
bring aboard some 705 survivors, several
of whom would die on the ship. Once it was
clear that there were no more escapees
to be rescued, the question became:
Where to go? One who had made it out
alive was White Star Line head J. Bruce
Ismay (who would be derided by the public
for surviving when so many women and
children had died). Rostron was decorous
enough to consult with Ismay before setting a course. The decision was made to
turn the *Carpathia*, a Cunard liner that had
been traveling between New York City and
Fiume in Austria-Hungary (the *Carpathia*'s
main duty was in the Mediterranean), and
head back to her port of origin—not least
because, with all the additional people now
on board, there were insufficient stores
to reach Europe and keep sustenance ade-
quate. The *Carpathia*, which had launched
back in 1902, was one of several ships
whose standard assignment was to fill up
with European immigrants and take them
to America, then to shuttle eastward with
wealthy Americans heading for a Grand
Tour holiday. So the clientele on this voyage was luxe. But taking signals from their
purposeful captain, the passengers issued
few or no complaints about the change
of plans, and most pitched in however they
could in the rescue, even though stewards
had been ordered by Rostron to keep the
Carpathia's 740 passengers separate from
the nearly equal number of *Titanic* survivors. On the opposite page: The survivors.
On this page, top: The arrival of the
Carpathia in New York City on April 18.
Bottom: The brave wireless operator,
Harold Bride, his frostbitten feet bandaged,
is assisted on the gangway in New York.
His superior in the Marconi Room, Jack
Phillips, made it off the stricken ship as
well, but perished during the night. We will
learn more of Phillips in our next chapter.

This is the first photograph made of the *Carpathia*, with the *Titanic*'s lifeboats draped off her side, arriving in New York City on Tuesday, April 18, after the dramatic rescue effort and four complicated days at sea. Rostron's performance throughout the crisis was topnotch and afterwards lauded by all: the passengers (a silver cup and a gold medal, presented by the unsinkable Maggie "Molly" Brown); the United States (a gold medal from the Shipwreck Society of New York, the Congressional Gold Medal, the Thanks of Congress and the American Cross of Honor); and of course Great Britain (a Liverpool Shipwreck and Humane Society medal and many other acknowledgments). Arthur Henry Rostron, who had been born in Lancashire, England, on May 14, 1869, first went to sea on the navy training ship *Conway* at age 13 and worked his way up on liners that allowed him to see the world: America, India, Australia. He joined the Cunard Line in 1895 and served on several ships prior to being made first officer of the *Lusitania* in 1907. Before he ever sailed on that ship, he was promoted to the captaincy of the *Brescia*. He was handed control of the *Carpathia* in early 1912, and quite soon thereafter was involved in the dramatic events of April 15. His ship arrived at the scene of the sinking at 3:30 a.m.; near 4 a.m., a green flare from one of the lifeboats was finally spotted. They took aboard the first of the survivors, from Lifeboat 2, at 4:10. More than four hours later, Lifeboat 12 was the last to be recovered. *Carpathia* arrived in New York City at night, and yet there were thousands waiting for her at Pier 54 off Little West 12th Street. There, on the Lower West Side of Manhattan, the Women's Relief Committee, the Council of Jewish Women, the Travelers Aid Society and others stepped forth to help, and the crew of the *Carpathia* was finally able to breathe. As the press descended and tales circulated, it became clear that here was a story of light against the dark horror: the heroism of the rescue ship and her captain. After testifying before Congress, Rostron was received by President Taft at the White House, who gave him a signed letter of thanks. And when he had completed the requisite tour of tribunals in England, Rostron returned to work. He moved on from the *Carpathia* in 1913, and during World War I commanded, among other ships, the *Lusitania* and the *Mauretania*. In 1915 he captained the *Aulania* in maneuvers during the brutal Battle of Gallipoli in Turkey. If he is forever associated with the *Carpathia*, his deepest relationship was with the *Mauretania*. He commanded this ship as a combat vessel (a troops transport) and then as a passenger liner until 1928; he led her on several record-breaking crossings of the Atlantic. Rostron became a Knight Commander of the Order of the British Empire in 1926. Sir Arthur left behind his life on the seas in 1931, worked on his memoirs, and died in 1940.

The *Carpathia* became a storied ship because of the rescue. Other boats had more gruesome assignments: the recovery of bodies, many of which were afloat because most passengers had donned life jackets. White Star Line chartered two cable-laying vessels out of Canada to perform the unhappy duty, and on a cold and clear April 17, the *Mackay-Bennett* pulled out of Halifax, Nova Scotia, with several tons of ice, scores of coffins, a minister from All Saints Cathedral and a master embalmer and his team. This ship worked the North Atlantic for several days, ultimately recovering more than 300 bodies, nearly half of which would be buried in Nova Scotia (others were too badly damaged for the return and were buried at sea). The *Mackay-Bennett* was joined by the *Minia*, aboard which there was a man with a camera. Top: A whaler from the *Minia* takes aboard a victim. Right: A body is readied on deck for its coffin. Above: Hearses are lined up on the Halifax wharf to transport *Titanic* victims recovered by the *Minia*.

In New York City, crowds gather in the many public squares, including Times Square, to get the very latest news about the dead and missing, and about what in the world had happened out there. The newspapers are ferocious in their competition for stories, and since every one of the survivors is somewhere in town, any energetic effort is rewarded. These reports will lead to the first draft of the legend of the *Titanic*. Such enduring tales as the courage of wireless operators Phillips and Bride were first written in this period—including one by Bride himself, who gave his account, in lengthy detail, to *The New York Times* (an account that was largely confirmed, thank goodness, by other survivors in the weeks and years ahead). "The Orphans of the Titanic" became a big story, as did the valiant efforts of the *Carpathia*'s crew and captain. Many of the men who had survived the sinking were instantly vilified, while the newly widowed women, including the pregnant Mrs. Astor, became heroines. Perhaps the most ink was spilled over Margaret Brown, the unsinkable one, who had tried to boss her lifeboat to do the right thing (it wasn't initially clear that she had not succeeded) and who became a kind of Dame of the *Titanic*. The forceful, fantastic (and rich!) "Molly" Brown, of whom we will learn more in our next chapter, rose to the occasion, and assumed "*Titanic* Commemoration" as the latest of her many good works. She saw immediately that New York City was becoming a big part of the story, and not long after the dust had cleared from the *Carpathia*'s arrival, she began work to have some kind of tangible memorial built. It took shape in 1913 as a 60-foot-tall lighthouse, funded by public subscription, that first stood high above the East River, extending upward from the roof of the Seamen's Church Institute of New York and New Jersey. In 1968 that organization changed locations, and the Titanic Memorial Lighthouse was donated to the South Street Seaport Museum. It stands today on the corner of Fulton and Pearl, directing interested passersby to New York's legacy in the *Titanic* saga.

Hundreds of Britishers, mostly members of *Titanic*'s crew, returned home on April 29 aboard the SS *Lapland,* which anchored beyond the harbor in Plymouth. From a contemporaneous account in the *Manchester Guardian:* "In the town, the church bells began to send out a sweet ringing over the water, and that must have been the first sound from shore to reach the ears of those on deck. We could see them dimly through the glass, leaning over the side and staring at the grey terraces of Plymouth, whence the homely smoke of breakfasts was rising." Left: The evacuees coming into port aboard a Great Western Railway ferry. Top: On May 1, men in a jury-rigged dormitory at Plymouth's Millbay docks, before they disperse to their several destinations. Above: On May 4, *Titanic* survivors are served dinner in a shed set aside for them at the Plymouth docks.

FPG/HULTON/GETTY

The anxiety of the survivors goes without saying, and most were still in deep emotional distress. The anxiety of those waiting for loved ones (top) was lesser only by degrees. At the gates just above is a crowd in Plymouth anticipating the arrival of the *Lapland* from New York, and at right are friends and relations of *Titanic* passengers in Southampton. This was, of course, the English port from which the ship had departed on her maiden voyage, and it was particularly hard hit. Most of the crew had lived in the city, and over 500 households lost at least one family member. According to the *Hampshire Chronicle* of April 20, almost a thousand local families were directly affected, and every street in the Chapel district lost more than one resident.

TOPICAL PRESS/GETTY (2)

The *Titanic* was not the first case of a massive tragedy inspiring a general outpouring of sympathy, but the aftermath of the sinking stands today as an early template for relief efforts held in reaction to such a tragedy, be it Bangladeshi flooding, Somalian famine or 9/11 violence. On April 29, opera stars Enrico Caruso and Mary Garden took part in special concerts that raised nearly $12,000 to benefit victims of the disaster (of course, "Songe d'Automne" and "Nearer My God to Thee" were on the program). "The hearts of men and women have been deeply touched, consciences have been awakened," read a contemporaneous account. "An impression was made on the multitudes to an extent never before exceeded." Memorial services and marches were held throughout Great Britain, and at many of these the Salvation Army passed the plate. British Salvationists raised more than £1,000 for the Titanic Disaster Widows and Orphans Distress Fund—equivalent to more than $300,000 today. The largest sum of money came from Southampton, the brutalized city that was the *Titanic*'s home port. Slum officer Ensign Palmer, who raised funds in that city, wrote: "On Saturday, the 20th, I spent three-and-a-half hours collecting for the Relief Fund, and never want to live again through such an experience. Thousands wept with us. We collected £30 10s; £20 of it in copper, and many hundreds of halfpennies were given by the poorest of the poor." The Salvationists played a part, and so did the Scouts (opposite, top). Children yearned to give or serve, whether in England (opposite, bottom left) or elsewhere (left, on the streets of Paris). The photograph at bottom right on the opposite page is of a different sort: It shows a *Titanic* survivor signing an autograph. The kind of fame that attached to the sinking of the *Titanic* spurred great charity, and also made celebrities—major or minor—of any who had been involved.

UNIVERSAL IMAGES/GETTY (2)

The U.S. inquiry: Chaired by Senator William Alden Smith (top) of Michigan, the hearings began at the Waldorf-Astoria Hotel in New York City (above and right) the day after the *Carpathia* arrived. British newspapers accused Smith of grandstanding and keeping English citizens from returning home quickly, but he remained resolute: "The calamity through which we have just passed has left traces of sorrow everywhere . . . this should be the occasion for a new birth of vigilance, and future generations must accord to this event a crowning motive for better things." His subcommittee's report led to reforms in international maritime safety.

GRANGER

The British inquiry: Chaired by Lord Mersey (top), the panel heard from members of the Leyland Line's *Californian* crew as well as passengers and crew from the *Titanic*. Left: Participants arrive at the Scottish Drill Hall in London on opening day, May 2; above is the daily bustle outside. The upshot of the investigation was, as had happened in the States, new regulations rather than penalties, but there was eye-opening testimony about how the lifeboat service had always been directed at First Class passengers. Most in steerage, who never saw the Boat Deck, didn't even know where the lifeboats were.

pposite: Precisely one week after the *Titanic* sank, a memorial Requiem Mass for the victims is said in St. Colman's Cathedral in Queenstown, Ireland—the ship's last-ever port of call. Above: In June, the wounds are still fresh in England, where this memorial is erected on the beach in Bournemouth. The commemorations, religious services, meetings and marches continued on through the late spring and summer of 1912. Postcards mourning the *Titanic* were issued, and songs were written; today, sheet music to "Be British" or "Wreck of the Titanic" are collectibles. So are limited-edition black teddy bears made in Germany to be given as mourning gifts; one of the bears sold at auction in 2000 for more than £91,000. There were events of remembrance that were smaller, more private. On May 31, Mrs. John Jacob Astor IV hosted at her Upper East Side town house in Manhattan two fellow *Titanic* widows and, from the *Carpathia,* Captain Rostron and surgeon Dr. Frank E. McGee. After the rescue at sea, Rostron had given over his cabin to the three women, and they, now all dressed in black, wanted to say thank you. Rostron and McGee's taxi from the pier to Mrs. Astor's home blew a tire, and then they had to survive a phalanx of photographers who had found out what was up, but once inside they enjoyed a gracious, heartfelt reunion. The following evening they were guests at a fund-raising concert at the Moulin Rouge that sought to ease the pain of the families of the *Titanic*'s suddenly legendary eight-man orchestra. Five hundred musicians from many New York area bands, plus members of the U.S. Army and U.S. Navy bands, took part. For a bit more on the *Titanic*'s orchestra, in particular its leader, please turn the page.

O n the pages just prior, we talked about Mrs. Astor and also about the *Titanic*'s band. At left is the funeral procession of John Jacob Astor IV in early May, with thousands lining the streets as he is brought into Trinity Church Cemetery and Mausoleum in upper Manhattan. Services were also performed in the small Episcopal Church of the Messiah in Rhinebeck, New York, where Astor had been born. At top is the funeral procession of Wallace Hartley, the *Titanic*'s heroic bandmaster, in Colne, Lancashire, England. Thirty thousand have turned out to honor their favorite son who had once sung in the church choir. Above is a *Titanic* section of one of three graveyards in Halifax where the recovered victims of the tragedy are buried—row upon row of black granite headstones, each bearing the indelible date April 15, 1912.

THE
VICTIMS

THE
SURVIVORS

There were four lovely, splendid days at sea for the passengers aboard *Titanic*, as we have seen in the chapter prior. The *Olympic*, in many ways *Titanic*'s twin, was also in the North Atlantic, having first launched the previous spring, and surely these four days, beginning on April 10, 1912, were the greatest in the history of the White Star Line's fleet of luxury ships. And then came the horrible night that would forever cement White Star's fame and its legacy.

On April 14, the consequential iceberg and others were certainly seen, looming. At 11:40 p.m., the consequential iceberg was struck. There was no immediate sense of alarm. Festivities on board continued as midnight approached. Down below, water gushed in; crewmen considered what that meant as they rushed to staunch the flood.

The mighty ship had been well built, and she listed only subtly in the early periods of her crisis. It became clear to those in charge, however, that evacuation was called for. They knew, as well, that the *Titanic* had sailed with one fatal flaw: too few lifeboats—enough for barely half of those on board. Who would be saved, and who might not? Particularly in the relatively calm first 90 minutes after the crash, before the outcome of the disaster became generally clear, many lifeboats tragically were launched with nowhere near a full complement of passengers. (Lifeboat 1 could accommodate 40, but left with only a dozen.) In this period, the protocol of "women and children first" was established and, for the most part, adhered to. By 2 a.m., the water had risen, desperation had set in, the last departing lifeboats were filled or overfilled, and the fateful end was at hand. Just before 2:20, the ship's stern rose in the air like a breaching whale, scores of people were flung into the sea, and the *Titanic* split in two and plunged.

The world would learn of the disaster later that morning, and then the stories would follow—stories of people, stories that humanized the tragedy. The *Titanic* disaster took on a face, a thousand faces and more.

Here, in the following pages, we see some of them.

On the pages immediately previous, Collapsible D approaches the *Carpathia* with only slightly more than two dozen survivors. Two of these, both toddlers, will become famous in *Titanic* lore, and we will meet the Navratil brothers more fully in this chapter, on page 120.

UNSINKABLE

Opposite is Margaret "Molly" Brown presenting a cup, in thanks, to the quick-acting *Carpathia* captain, Arthur Henry Rostron. The "Unsinkable Molly," who would be immortalized onscreen by actresses from Debbie Reynolds to Kathy Bates, was a piece of work even without any Hollywood embellishment. Born in Hannibal, Missouri, to Irish immigrants, Maggie (not, actually, "Molly") Tobin hoped to marry rich but did the opposite—and then her husband, the self-educated J.J. Brown, hit it big in mining. Suddenly Maggie was a wealthy socialite, and then a philanthropist and an activist: She was an early feminist and campaigned for the rights of children. She and her husband had separated by the time she traveled on the *Titanic*, and she was very much on her own in Lifeboat 6. Maggie Brown, who took an oar at one point, vigorously urged that the boat return for possible other survivors. Although legend holds that it did so, sturdier accounts have Quartermaster Robert Hichens, who was in charge of the rescue vessel, refusing Brown's demand as he believed any swimmers were already dead and that they themselves could be pulled down by the *Titanic*'s suction.

GRANGER

"THE ASTORS WERE ABOARD!"

★

That was the news that flashed from point to point, mouth to ear, in New York City when it was learned that the *Titanic* had gone down. As ever, the hoi polloi as well as high society found themselves riveted by the elite: *The Astors were aboard!* This was John Jacob Astor IV, the contemporary head of one of America's great families and fortunes, and his young (and second) wife, Madeleine, as well as their Airedale, Kitty (left, in New York City). Was Mrs. Astor alive? How had Colonel Astor (he had been appointed during the Spanish-American War) acted? She was among the living, in fact, and he had behaved properly. As the movies have it, there was apparently a late-night session in the gymnasium, during which John tried to assure Madeleine that all would be well. Not long thereafter, Astor gave his wife over to Second Officer Charles Lightoller, who was supervising the boarding of Lifeboat 4. Astor did ask if he might join his wife and maid since Madeleine was in "a delicate condition." Lightoller reminded him that the protocol remained women and children first, and Astor stepped back. He and Kitty died that night. Madeleine returned to the United States, and gave birth to her and John's son, John Jacob VI, who is seen opposite, circa 1935, as a handsome young man with no fear of the sea, posing on the SS *Leviathan*.

TOPICAL PRESS/GETTY

SINNER AND SAINT?

H ere is neither a villain nor any kind of hero, although for decades that is the way these two men have been portrayed, especially when they are counterbalanced against one another on the same page, as they are here. As with everything in life, the truth is more complicated. But it is fact that Bruce Ismay, chairman of the White Star Line (seen above, center, coming down the gangway of the *Adriatic* at the Custom House in Liverpool, having returned from New York City and his appearance before the U.S. *Titanic* inquiry) survived the sinking, while Thomas Andrews (left), the ship's architect who knew immediately what the iceberg damage meant, died. Did Ismay, during the voyage, encourage Captain Smith to travel faster through the ice field, so as to make news upon reaching New York City? Was Andrews a voice of reason on board, one who knew what the ship was capable of—and vulnerable to? Finally: Are these questions that are no longer worth asking? That is quite possibly the case, but Ismay and Andrews will never be allowed to rest easily. The former was, after all, one of the adult men who lived—and all of them were suspect for the rest of their days. The latter was a more complex case. Andrews helped build this thing, and she sank, taking many lives with her. Historical reports are that he was conflicted, or troubled, or doubtful. Was any of this why, when the ship was sinking, he resolutely chose to go down with her—last seen in the Smoking Room, having forsaken his life jacket, staring into space.

GRANGER

THE MEN OF THE WHITE STAR LINE

elow are stewards who survived the sinking, waiting in London to be called before the British Board of Trade inquiry; at bottom is a team photograph of the *Olympic's* engineering officers, 14 of whom (numbered in the picture) would transfer to the *Titanic*—and perish in the disaster. Of the 908 total crew on the ship, 701

were lost—they did not have priority on the lifeboats. The U.S. Senate hearings into the tragedy began soon after *Carpathia* landed in New York and continued from April 19 to May 25; their British counterparts ran from May 2 until July 3. Among the things investigated were the dearth of lifeboats; whether the route chosen across the North

Atlantic was ill-advised; whether the ship was traveling too fast; and whether the crew behaved properly. The Board of Trade cleared White Star of culpability, but this was done in part because of fears that lawsuits could injure the company, and that customers would flee British luxury liners in favor of French and German competitors.

TOPICAL PRESS/GETTY

UNIVERSAL IMAGES/GETTY

PLAYERS IN THE DRAMA

★

There were more than 2,000 compelling stories being written that night, each as meaningful as the next. Uncommon expressions of astuteness, valor, grace, insensitivity, compassion or lack of compassion would be recounted a thousand times in the days and decades ahead. Here are four men, two of whom died and two of whom survived. At left is a final photograph of Captain Smith. A survivor

claimed Smith leapt into the sea as his ship went under; two others said they saw him swimming; *Titanic* lore has him exhorting his fellows to make for the lifeboats but to always "Be British!" A star witness at both post-disaster inquiries would be Second Officer Charles Lightoller, who had helped load the lifeboats, and he steadfastly defended the behavior of Captain Smith during the crisis, as well as that of wireless operators Jack Phillips (opposite, left) and Harold Bride who, as we have mentioned earlier, stayed at their posts until the last possible moment. Phillips and Bride did finally flee and then separate, Phillips heading aft; he would die. Bride helped others wrestle with Collapsible B; suddenly it was washed overboard. He grasped an oarlock and was swept from the ship with the lifeboat; he found himself beneath the overturned boat and was able to swim out and clamber aboard. Later, on the *Carpathia*, despite suffering severe frostbite, he helped radio the hundreds of messages that were sent forth. The young man in the flat cap (opposite) is lookout Frederick Fleet, who, at 11:39 p.m. on April 14, had first spotted from his vantage in the crow's nest the thing that would cause *Titanic*'s doom, had rung the warning bell three times, and had telephoned the bridge: "Iceberg right ahead!" Emergency maneuvers were taken, the *Titanic* began to turn slowly—but it was too late. Fleet survived the sinking, eventually became a night watchman and died by his own hand many years later, in 1965. At right is Second Class passenger Stuart Collett, who also survived. The Englishman was a 25-year-old theology student when he traveled on the *Titanic*. According to at least one contemporaneous press account, on the fateful Sunday the "boy preacher" had assisted in the ship's religious service, attended by three dozen, at which the sending hymn was "Now the Day Is Ended."

TOPICAL PRESS/GETTY

ETERNAL LOVE

The *Titanic* story of Isidor and Ida Straus (below) in no way equates with that of Ben Guggenheim except, perhaps, in its high passion. The Strauses, too, were of New York City's uppermost crust: He was, in 1912, co-owner (with his brother) of Macy's department store, and was a former Democratic member of the U.S. House of Representatives. By 1912, he and Ida had been married more than 40 years and had built a large family that included six children (a seventh had died in infancy). The Strauses were known by their friends to be intensely devoted to one another; if ever they were parted, they wrote each other letters every day. And so it was on the Boat Deck. Ida was offered a place in Lifeboat 8. Isidor, too, would have been allowed to board the half-filled vessel but declined as there were still many women to be saved; he sent his wife's maid forward. Ida then turned resolute: "We have been living together many years. Where you go, I go." Survivors said the Strauses were sitting in deck chairs, holding hands, when a wave washed them out to sea.

DRESSING FOR DISASTER

Above are Benjamin Guggenheim and his wife, the former Florette Seligman, circa 1910. He was the fifth of seven sons of Meyer Guggenheim, who had made an enormous fortune in mining and smelting. If the Guggenheims could be seen to rival the Astors in American high society, Benjamin's death on the *Titanic* did not command the headlines that John Astor's did. There was a reason for this. Guggenheim, as was his habit in this period, had been traveling with a woman who was not his wife—and that wasn't the kind of angle that helped romanticize the *Titanic* story. Later, however, when details of Guggenheim's extravagant behavior as he went down with the ship were related, he became a character who was indispensable to novelists and moviemakers. Guggenheim had boarded the ship with an entourage including his mistress, the French singer Léontine Aubart; his valet, Victor Giglio; his chauffeur, René Pernot; and Aubart's maid, Emma Sägesser. The women felt the jolt when the *Titanic* collided with the iceberg, and woke Giglio and Guggenheim (Pernot was ensconced in Second Class; he would perish at sea that night). On the Boat Deck, Aubart and Sägesser were given places in Lifeboat 9. Guggenheim sought to calm the women's distress, telling Sägesser in German, "We will soon see each other again! It's just a repair. Tomorrow the *Titanic* will go on again." He knew he was dissembling. With Giglio in tow, he returned to his First Class accommodations having made the decision to die in style. He and his valet changed into their finest evening wear, then repaired to a room off the grand staircase to enjoy brandy and a final cigar. "We've dressed up in our best and are prepared to go down like gentlemen," he said to a *Titanic* steward who survived, and he gave him this message: "Tell my wife, if it should happen that my secretary and I both go down, tell her I played the game out straight to the end. No woman shall be left aboard this ship because Ben Guggenheim is a coward."

STRAUS HISTORICAL SOCIETY

COURTESY HOSONO FAMILY

THE RING

⋆

Why do we know more of Elin Gerda and Edvard Lindell than we do of so many other unfortunates from Third Class? Because of a ring. Newlyweds when they left Helsingborg, Sweden, to start a new life in Connecticut, they were among those from steerage who managed to get to the Boat Deck in the ship's final moments. They slid down the rapidly sloping deck, plunged into the sea and made their way toward Collapsible A. Edvard was able to get aboard, only to die soon. Another Swede from Third Class, August Wennerström, who would survive, tried to pull Elin into the boat and grasped her hand for as long as he could, but ultimately he could hold on no longer and she drifted away. Collapsible A was abandoned at sea (its passengers transferred to Lifeboat 14), and weeks later, the White Star liner *Oceanic* discovered it adrift. A gold ring, inscribed "Edvard and Gerda," was found in the boat. The ring was traced to Mrs. Lindell and returned to her family. Because of this poetic footnote, the larger story was pieced together and continues to be told.

MOMENT OF TRUTH

⋆

"Fine weather," Second Class passenger Masabumi Hosono, who is pictured here with his wife, Toyo, wrote in his diary regarding his day on the *Titanic*: "Spent the day reading, exercising and napping." Later: "I was almost drowsing when I felt the slight sensation of the ship's hitting something, but did not take it seriously." He would apprehend the urgency soon enough, and the father of four, whose family was back home in Japan, would find himself facing the ultimate decision: certain death at sea, or a chance at survival. "Thus, I made the jump for the lifeboat." Perhaps he knew, even as he helped row toward salvation, what consequences awaited him in his homeland. In a culture that honors sacrifice, Hosono was branded a coward and barraged with hate mail. He lost his job at the Ministry of Transportation, and retreated into his art collection and Buddhist readings. His and Toyo's family grew to six children, but at home one subject was never discussed: *Titanic*.

BUREAU L A COLLECTION/SYGMA/CORBIS

ON COLLAPSIBLE B

The last lifeboat to hit the water in *Titanic*'s final moments was Collapsible B, and it floated off the deck upside down, which is how it would remain until found the next morning. A 47-year-old British justice of the peace, Algernon Barkworth, was one of nearly 30 who pulled themselves onto the boat's back. He dictated his experience upon being rescued (he could not write as his hands had been frozen): "I climbed up on the Boat Deck railing and dropped about 30 feet into the sea . . . When I came up, I swam for all I was worth to get away from the sinking ship . . . Looking over my shoulder I saw the *Titanic* disappear with a volley of loud reports so I swam slowly around and came luckily up on an overturned lifeboat. I climbed up on this at this time. The screams of the drowning was most terrible. Several more people climbed up the stern of our boat, which was now full. We 'competed' to keep everyone else from gathering upon. We drifted until daybreak . . . When we were rescued the water was up over our knees. We had two dead men on our stern, one of which fell off. The other one was taken aboard the *Carpathia* and was afterwards buried. When taken aboard, we were treated most kindly."

THE GREAT MAN

If in the U.S. the news was that Astor had been lost, in England the largest headlines reported the death of William Thomas Stead. A crusading journalist and editor, his personal causes included world peace, women's rights, civil liberties and the plight of the impoverished. He was traveling to New York at the invitation of William Howard Taft to participate in a peace congress at Carnegie Hall. (News circulated later that he may have been due to receive the 1912 Nobel Peace Prize.) As the *Titanic* struggled, Stead aided women and children into lifeboats, then repaired to the First Class Smoking Room, made himself comfortable in a leather chair, began reading and awaited his fate. Among the odder facts about Stead was that he was a dedicated spiritualist, and an eerie thing about his career in writing is that, in 1886, he published a cautionary sketch about a mail steamer that sinks in the mid-Atlantic with great loss of life due to a lack of lifeboats.

THE LUCKY MAN

The *Titanic* seemed such a thoroughly British enterprise—registered in Liverpool, a crew of Brits from Captain Smith on down—but it was in fact an American-owned ship. The White Star Line was one of several maritime transportation firms whose controlling trust was the International Mercantile Marine Company. The founding owner of the IMMC was none other than the Wall Street titan J.P. Morgan, who also owned U.S. Steel, General Electric and numerous banks. Morgan was a man of prodigious passions: for art collecting, for outsize cigars, for the sea. He was an avid yachtsman, and it was he who legendarily said about one of the boats in his splendid personal fleet: "If you have to ask the price, you can't afford it." Morgan was scheduled to travel on the maiden voyage of White Star's marvelous new *Titanic;* reserved for him was a suite with its own private Promenade Deck. Before boarding, Morgan had a change of plans, either because he took ill or simply decided to extend his stay in Europe. The financier's good fortune bought him barely another year, however, and he died in his sleep in March 1913, just shy of his seventy-sixth birthday.

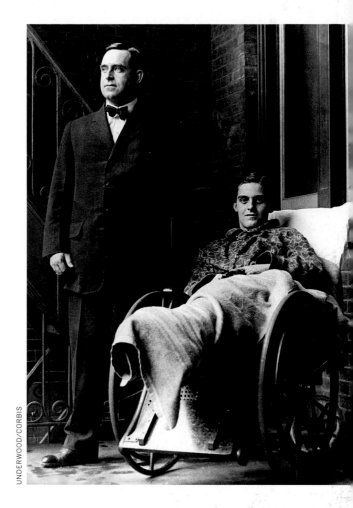

ANOTHER FROM BOAT B

Algernon Barkworth, on the facing page, testified candidly that those who were first on the overturned Collapsible B "competed" to keep others off. One of those apparently was Thomas Whiteley, a steward in First Class whose leg had been broken when he got caught in the ropes as lifeboats were being lowered. (Above: Whiteley convalescing.) The 18-year-old Londoner talked to the *New York Tribune* shortly after arriving in the States, and recalled that after his accident on the Boat Deck, "In some way I got overboard . . . I drifted near a boat wrong side up. About thirty men were clinging to it. They refused to let me get on. Someone tried to hit me with an oar, but I scrambled on to her." The earlier rule of the sea—"women and children first"—had yielded at this desperate point to "every man for himself."

HONEYMOON'S END

The American Mary Farquharson (above) was 18 and Daniel Marvin 19 when they wed in 1912. Wealthy children of New York society, they decided to honeymoon in Europe. They had a lovely time, and were returning home on the *Titanic* in First Class. Mary clung to her husband during the perilous night, but he finally insisted she board the lifeboat: "It's all right, little girl. You go. I will stay." He did, and died. Back home, Mary was one of three women survivors to give birth to a child after the disaster: Mary Margaret Elizabeth Marvin.

A WOMAN OF PARTS

Helen Churchill Hungerford Candee could do it all—she was a writer, an activist, a socialite, an interior decorator, a geographer, a single mother, a horse-woman (here at the head of a women's suffrage parade in Washington, D.C., on March 3, 1913) and, obviously, a survivor. Her first book, a best-seller in 1900, was *How Women May Earn a Living*, and she did so not long thereafter by becoming one of the first American professional interior decorators, with clients including President Teddy Roosevelt. She was finishing up *The Tapestry Book* in Europe in 1912 when she received word that her son had been hurt in an accident, so she rushed home—the quickest available passage being on the *Titanic.* Though she broke her ankle on Lifeboat 6 and had to walk with a cane for much of the next year, she was back on the horse in Washington the following spring.

MRS. MORGAN?

The woman at left is remembered by history and was known in her time as Lady Duff-Gordon. She was sailing with her aristocratic sportsman husband, the Scotsman Sir Cosmo Duff-Gordon. But they were not traveling as the Duff-Gordons but rather as Mr. and Mrs. Morgan, perhaps because the lady's fashion house—she was one of the very most successful dress designers of the day—was wary of U.S. Customs. Cosmo escaped with his wife in a lifeboat with only three other passengers and seven crewmen aboard; it was later alleged that he had bribed the rowers to pull away from others who were drowning.

A BETTER LIFE

Clear Annie Cameron, daughter of a tailor, was 35 years old and working as a personal maid in London when she decided to head for America, land of opportunity. She conspired with a friend, Nellie Walcroft, to flee. They booked passage on an ocean liner, then found themselves transferred to the *Titanic;* their Second Class accommodations cost them each £21. On the night of April 14, Nellie woke her friend: "Clear, what's that?" They listened, and someone outside their cabin on E Deck yelled, "An iceberg!" On the Boat Deck, Fifth Officer Harold Lowe was shooting his revolver to keep anxious men from getting onto Lifeboat 14, which the women boarded. Their night was hardly over: Lowe, who was in charge of 14, wanted to return for other survivors, so he gathered lifeboats together, transferred passengers (Cameron and Walcroft ended up on Lifeboat 10), and went back to the terrible site of the sinking. Lowe's boat took on four additional people, one of whom died. Cameron made it to New York, where she went to work . . . as a maid.

FRANK FINDLAY

THE ACTRESS

The sinking of the *Titanic* was screen-worthy even before all the survivors' stories had been told. This woman was there: Dorothy Gibson was a 22-year-old silent screen actress going home with her mother from a six-week vacation in Italy. The women, traveling in First Class (Gibson was, for a brief time, among filmdom's highest-paid actresses), were playing bridge when the iceberg was struck. Dorothy and her mother were two of only 28 aboard the capacity-65 Lifeboat 7, which was the first boat lowered at 12:45 a.m. Very soon after arriving in New York aboard the *Carpathia,* Gibson co-wrote and starred in a quickie one-reeler, *Saved from the Titanic,* wearing the very dress and coat that she wore when boarding the lifeboat. This was the first of several *Titanic* box-office smashes, a hit in the United States, England and France. The last remaining prints of the film were destroyed in a 1914 fire at Éclair Studios, in Fort Lee, New Jersey, and their loss is today considered one of the greatest in film history.

NOBILITY

Lucy-Nöel Martha, Countess of Rothes (below), was on her way to meet her husband in North America. A *Titanic* survivor whose actions are attested to by those who were with her, she stands these many years later as an exemplary figure. There was valorous behavior on *Titanic's* deck, as we have seen, but in the lifeboats (as we have also seen) there were problems. Consider: Of lifeboats with capacities of 65 each, Number 7 left with 28 people and didn't return; Number 6 also left with 28; Number 8 left with 32. The countess was on Number 8, and she, her cousin Gladys Cherry, Seaman Thomas Jones and an American woman insisted that they should return for other survivors. They were overruled by the majority. "Ladies," Jones said, "if any of us are saved, remember I wanted to go back. I would rather drown with them than leave them." At times during the night, the countess steered Lifeboat 8, and Gladys rowed. Nobility, as reflected in actions this night, was democratic: Some in First Class behaved exceptionally, some terribly, and the same was true in steerage.

PA

UNIVERSAL IMAGES/GETTY

TONI LOPEZ/SIPA

ESCAPE FROM STEERAGE

Second from left, below, is Anna Kincaid, with her American family. She is the former Anna Sofia Sjöblom of Finland, who was just about to turn 18 as she set out on a long journey to see her father, who was working for a timber company in Olympia, Washington. Anna and three other young Finns were to travel aboard the White Star liner *Adriatic,* but they, like others, were transferred to the *Titanic* because of a coal strike. For a bit less than £7 each, Anna and her friends would be part of history: the maiden voyage of the world's grandest ship (albeit in the confines of Third Class). She was excited, certainly, but this was mitigated by constant seasickness; on her birthday, April 14, she hardly reveled. When the ship hit the iceberg, she was fully dressed on her bed, not feeling well. Soon, of course, she was in action. At one point Anna and her companions, making their way to the upper decks, were confronted by metal gates across the stairways. They broke a window and made their way up the outside of the listing ship, climbing over the rail to the Boat Deck. A ship's officer put Anna in Lifeboat 16, which launched at 1:35 with 37 passengers (capacity 65). Her three friends died. Anna eventually reached the Pacific Northwest, remained there, married Gordon Kincaid, raised two children and passed away on November 3, 1975: a normal American life, with an interesting prologue.

THE ORPHANS

One of the most sensational stories to emerge in the aftermath of the catastrophe was that of the Navratil brothers, seen here just before they boarded the *Titanic*. Their father, Michel, had absconded with them, leaving his wife, from whom he was separated, in France. He boarded the America-bound liner with his boys, under the family name "Hoffman." In the *Titanic*'s final minutes, Second Officer Lightoller ordered his crew to form a tight ring around the last lifeboat to launch in order to keep men out and allow only women and children to board. Navratil thrust his sons, Michel Jr. (left) and Edmond, through the circle and they were put aboard Collapsible D. "I don't recall being afraid, I remember the pleasure, really, of going plop! Into the lifeboat," Michel recalled years later. "We ended up next to the daughter of an American banker who managed to save her dog—no one objected. There were vast differences of people's wealth on the ship, and I realized later that if we hadn't been in Second Class, we'd have died. The people who came out alive often cheated and were aggressive. The honest didn't stand a chance." The Navratils were the only children to reach the *Carpathia* without an adult guardian, and in New York, newspapers trumpeted the story of "The Orphans of the Titanic." Their mother was located, and White Star brought her from France for a tearful reunion in the United States on May 16. Later in life, Edmond became an interior decorator and architect, and served in the French Army during World War II. Michel, who had been three years old in 1912, grew to become a prominent philosopher and incidentally the last male survivor of the *Titanic*. Late in life, he returned to the United States for the first time since 1912, met with others who had sailed on the *Titanic,* and then visited his father's grave in Nova Scotia. He died in 2001.

COURTESY MILLVINA DEAN

AP

THE LAST SURVIVOR

★

So many tales that attach to *Titanic* seem storybook—too pat, stranger than fiction. And now we return to Millvina Dean, whom we met on page 116 as the *Titanic*'s youngest passenger, and who lived to be the oldest survivor. As the photograph at left implies, while she, her mother, Georgetta, and her older brother, Bertram Jr., survived, her father died—though she wasn't told this until she was eight years old. This picture was taken in the garden of Millvina's grandfather's property in England, and that's part of the story: The Deans had been destined for a new life in America, but Georgetta, destitute and surely in a daze, took her family home after they had spent two weeks recovering in a New York City hospital. Georgetta remarried but was never again well, retiring many afternoons with a headache. Millvina became a secretary, and worked till 1972, her final job being in Southampton—whence *Titanic* had sailed. She died on May 31, 2009, quite nearly a century after the great ship had pulled out of port. And with that, all who had sailed on *Titanic* were gone.

A NIGHT TO REMEMBER
REMEMBERED

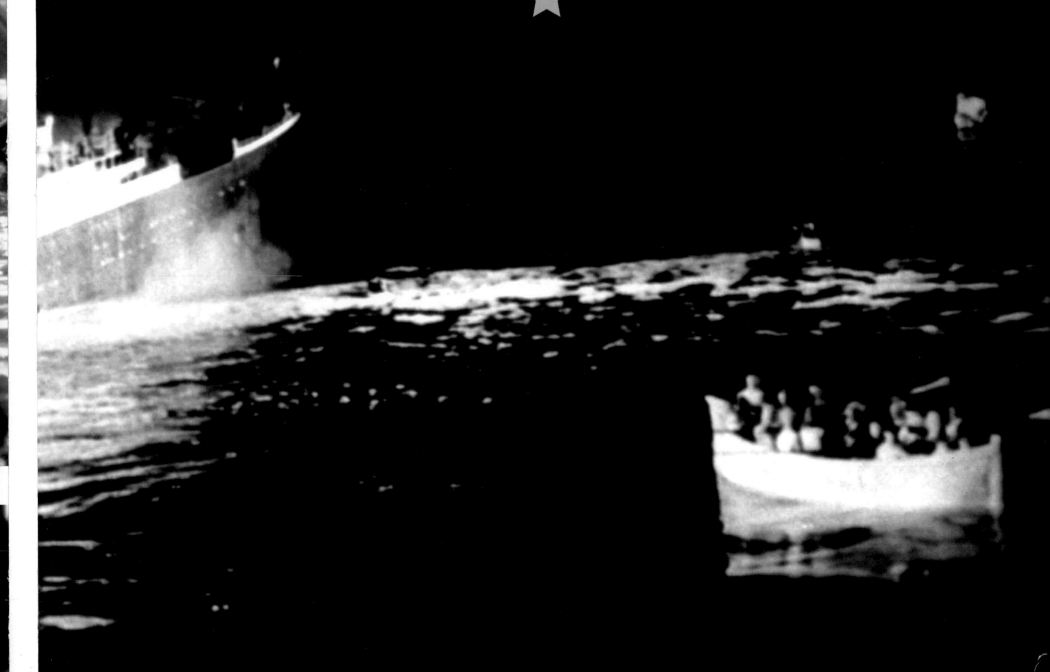

WALTER WANGER presents

Charles **BOYER** Jean **ARTHUR**

HISTORY IS MADE at NIGHT

LEO CARRILLO
COLIN CLIVE

TITA

SYBILLE SCH
CHARLOTTE TR
KERSTIN HEI
KARL SCHÖN
HANS NIEL
OTTO WERN

WINNE
11 ACADEMY AWAR
including
BEST PICTU

LEONARDO DiCAPRIO

ALL THE DRAMATIC
EXCITEMENT THE
SCREEN CAN HOLD!

TITANIC

Clifton **WEBB** · Barbara **STANWYCK**

ROBERT WAGNER · AUBREY DALTON · THELMA RITTER
BRIAN AHERNE · RICHARD BASEHART

TOBIS

ere, a plethora of print materials, including movie posters, a sampling of books and even a bit of sheet music. Fascinating facts: The 1943 German movie called *Titanic* (right) was a Nazi propaganda film meant to illustrate the evils of American and British capitalism and the bravery of German men. Also on this page: In the credits for a 1953 American film of the same name, we find Robert Wagner and Richard Basehart. There are ironies, tragic and not. Wagner was on a yacht off California's Catalina Island in 1981 when his wife, the actress Natalie Wood, drowned in the Pacific. And Basehart's most enduring fame with the American audience rests on two seafaring roles: that of Ishmael in the classic *Moby Dick,* and that of Admiral Harriman Nelson in the popular mid-'60s TV series *Voyage to the Bottom of the Sea.*

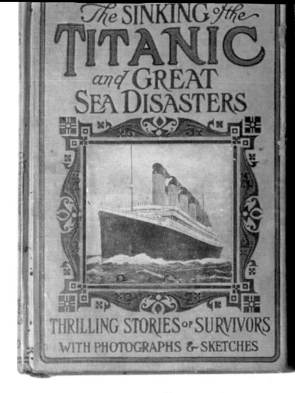

The SINKING of the **TITANIC** and GREAT SEA DISASTERS

THRILLING STORIES of SURVIVORS WITH PHOTOGRAPHS & SKETCHES

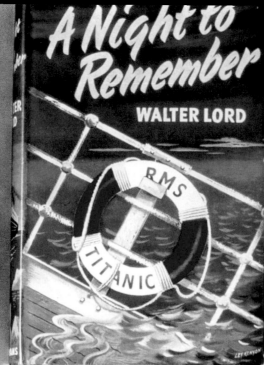

A **Night to Remember**

WALTER LORD

RMS TITANIC

The **TITANIC** and the **CALIFORNIAN**

FIELD

TITANIC...
THE GREATEST SEA DRAMA IN LIVING MEMORY

ORGANISATION PRESENTS WITH PRIDE

ETH **MORE** IN

HT TO REMEMBER

From the book by Walter Lord
Screenplay by Eric Ambler
Produced by William MacQuitty
Directed b

MY FATHER

BY ESTELLE.W. STEAD

SINKING of the **TITANIC**

"WOMEN AND CHILDREN FIRST"

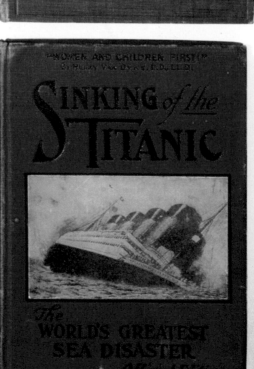

THE WORLD'S GREATEST SEA DISASTER

THE WRECK OF THE TITANIC

A DESCRIPTIVE PIANO COMPOSITION BY **JEANETTE FORREST**

60

Frank K. Root & Co.
CHICAGO — NEW YORK

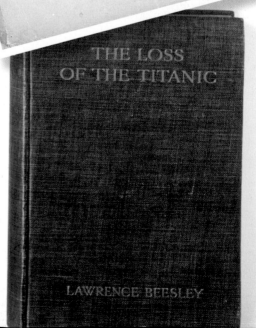

THE LOSS OF THE TITANIC

LAWRENCE BEESLEY

AT
REST

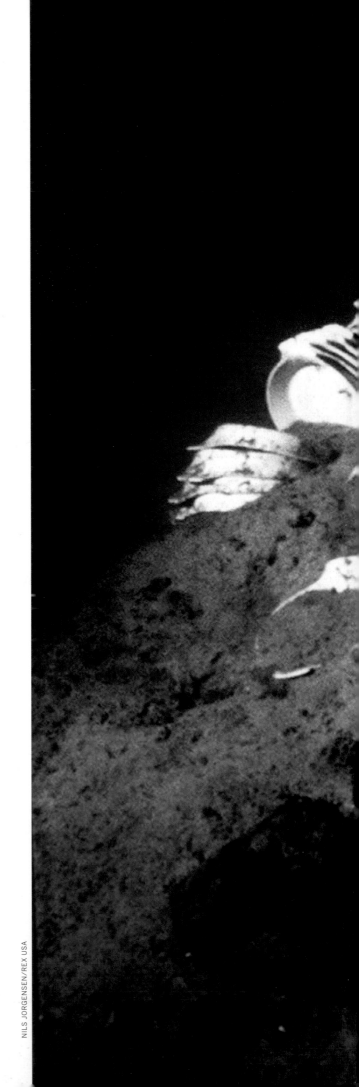

For 73 years, the *Titanic* slept undisturbed (except by natural forces) under approximately 12,460 feet of cold Atlantic seawater. Attempts were made to find the ship's remains, certainly, but they were unavailing.

In the late summer of 1985, the ship was found by a joint French-American team on an experimental expedition testing a deep-towed sonar-and-video system called Argo that it hoped would be effective in surveying deep-sea ridges. The crew of the research vessel *Knorr*, out of the Woods Hole Oceanographic Institution in Massachusetts, was definitely hoping to find the *Titanic*, but was equally interested in how Argo functioned. By the early morning hours of September 1— very near the same hour the ship had sunk in 1912—the researchers were already well content that Argo was a talented little machine. And then, about 230 miles south of Nova Scotia, it found the *Titanic*.

Those on board the *Knorr* were elated, of course, but expedition coleader Dr. Robert D. Ballard, head of Woods Hole's Deep Submergence Laboratory, set just the right tone when he radioed home to Cape Cod, "We're obviously very pleased and excited to have found the *Titanic*, but we are also very aware of the significance of the *Titanic* as a maritime disaster." Members of the *Knorr*'s crew gathered on the ship's fantail and staged a brief memorial service for those who had died 73 years earlier.

The Argo went on, later that year, to successfully study deep-sea mountain ranges. Bob Ballard went on to celebrity as a scientific "Mr. Titanic," as he and others continued to explore and photograph the wreck through the years. The ship and her compelling story surged once again to the fore of the world's imagination. And not too many years thereafter, James Cameron went to work.

On the previous pages: The rusted prow. At right, chinaware as neatly arrayed as could be imagined. Ballard made a two-and-a-half-hour descent in the mini-submarine *Alvin* in July 1986, 10 months after his original discovery, and saw some of this firsthand. But most of the photography on these and the following pages was taken later, during other expeditions, with advanced cameras and techniques.

★

NILS JORGENSEN/REX USA

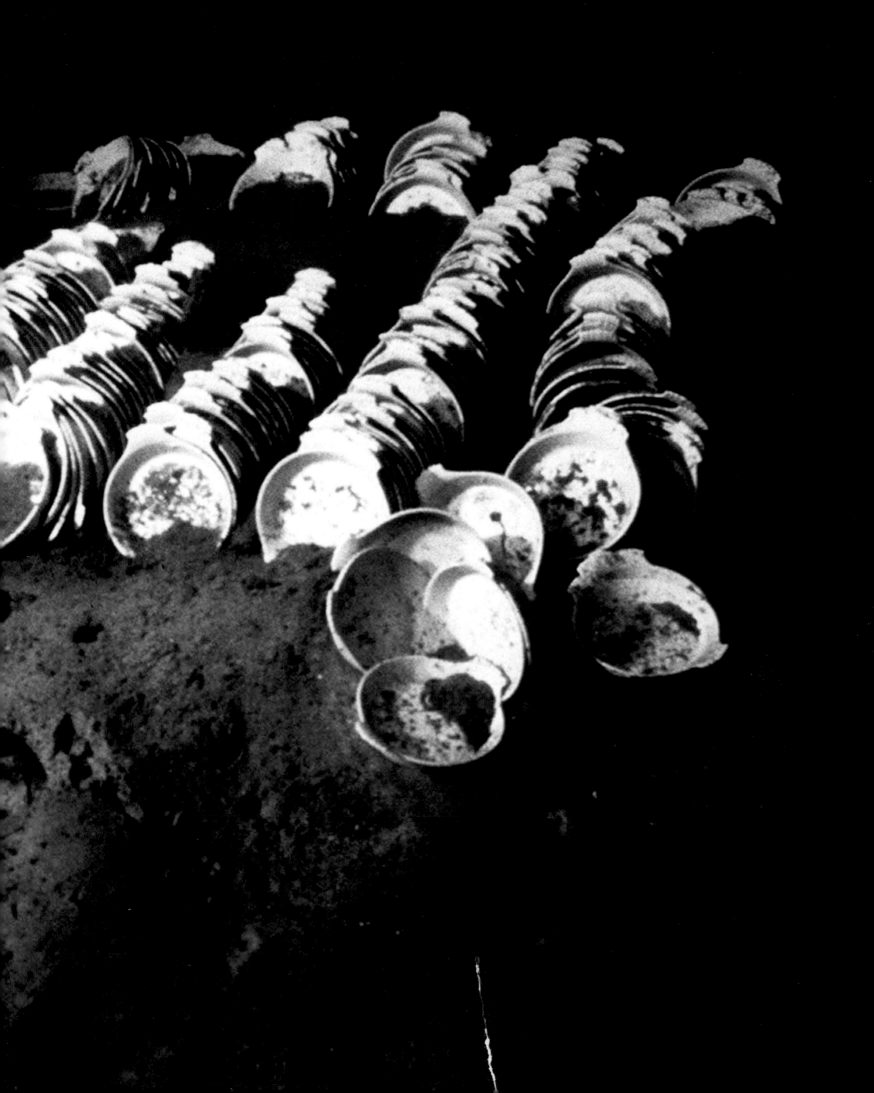

This is a corner of the Boat Deck directly opposite where Lifeboat 5 was stored and where many men no doubt stood and watched their loved ones lowered to the dark sea below. There is an obvious poignancy to these pictures, and to the fact that recent revisits to the site have confirmed that the *Titanic*'s shell is deteriorating much faster than earlier researchers suspected. Recently, the crow's nest from which Frederick Fleet had cried "Iceberg right ahead!" collapsed. "Rusticles"—a name Ballard gave to the strands of rust formed as bacteria eats away at the ship's hull and leaves its waste—are everywhere. There's little to be done about this, of course, beyond perhaps visiting the site less. That is Ballard's wish. He and his team bestowed on the wreck two commemorative plaques, one to the memory of the dead, the other asking future expeditions to leave the *Titanic*, which he considers a gravesite, undisturbed. But the *Titanic* wreckage rests in international waters, and RMS Titanic Inc.—no friend of Ballard's—has the right to salvage it. There have been eight major RMS Titanic Inc. expeditions since 1987, and some 5,500 items have been retrieved from the wreck. Statues, the crow's nest bell, luggage, light fixtures: They've all found their way back to the surface, where the finders claim careful stewardship. Millions of people have enjoyed the company's traveling show, *Titanic: The Artifact Exhibition*, but sometimes the audience gets confused. *Titanic* fans know that hundreds of other items have made their way to auction houses, where a vibrant *Titanic*-artifact industry flourishes. What's the difference between the items exhibited and those auctioned? Please turn the page.

In 1912 items were recovered floating in the water, in the bottoms of lifeboats or in the coat pockets of victims; most of these were returned to the families of the deceased, while others were kept by the finders. Many of those privately held items have been auctioned in recent years as *Titanic* memorabilia has grown in value. For instance: The pocket watch below, right, stopped at 2:16, is the one that belonged to steward Edmund Stone (please see page 60); it was found when he was found, and it commanded £94,000 (approximately $150,000 today) when the gavel landed at Henry Aldridge & Son Auctioneers in Wiltshire, England, in 2008—the highest price yet paid for a *Titanic* artifact. The other pieces here are self-explanatory, and were either salvaged a century ago or much more recently by RMS Titanic Inc., which now uses the name of its parent firm, Premier Exhibitions Inc. (The five-dollar bank note, for example, was in the purser's bag retrieved from the wreck.) Additionally, we have playing cards, a ship's chronometer, a purse, a comb, sheet music, a spoon and a pair of leather shoes, believed to have belonged to the Unknown Child (please see page 119). The boy, whose body was recovered by the crew of the *Mackay-Bennett* a few days after the tragedy, was, as we have said, buried in the Fairview Lawn Cemetery in Halifax. Meantime, the Halifax police were given an order to guard the belongings of victims, then later told to burn many to deter the hovering souvenir hunters. Clarence Northover, a sergeant in the force, grew emotional when he came to the small shoes, and he put them in a desk drawer in the police station. Northover moved to Ontario in 1919 and took the shoes with him. In 2002 his grandson Earle determined they belonged back in Halifax and donated them to the local museum there.

The *Titanic* was no fly-by-night affair for movie director James Cameron. The photograph of the intact Tiffany window at left and of the chandelier dangling from its wires, opposite, in an opening where once twirled a grand staircase were taken while Cameron was filming a documentary follow-up to his masterwork feature film. *Ghosts of the Abyss,* released in 2003 by Walt Disney, represented a kind of pilgrimage for Cameron, as, in the summer of 2001, he and a group of scientists made a dozen dives in two Russian submersibles, *Mir 1* and *Mir 2,* and came back with fantastic, emotionally charged imagery. *Ghosts of the Abyss,* which was Disney's first-ever full-length 3-D IMAX production, will be the largely forgotten interlude between the original *Titanic* of 15 years ago and the enhanced version now being released. But it is a powerful document, made all the more so for being factual. Opposite, bottom: Another emotionally charged photograph, this one from 1991. This is a close view of the forward port position, from which the last lifeboat was launched (that's a fallen lifeboat davit, left). The cylindrical object in the right half of the picture is the tip of the ship's toppled foremast.

Clockwise from the opposite page: A deck bench, a propeller, a porthole. When the *Titanic* was found, an age-old notion that it should or might be raised to the surface was floated once more. This will almost surely never happen. First of all, descendants of many victims realize there were no human remains found down there—they had all deteriorated or been swept away—and feel that the *Titanic*, as it now exists, should be the gravestone. (Survivor Eva Hart spoke for many when she called the salvagers "fortune hunters, vultures, pirates.") And then there are the physical problems. Much of what's left of the bow section, which plunged straight to the bottom, is today buried in more than 60 feet of mud. The stern imploded on its way down. It is thought that, even with modern technologies, any effort to bring a substantial portion of the ship up from 12,460 feet in its deteriorated state would cause it to crumble. So the *Titanic* will most probably stay where it is, nurturing within its hull the mixed community of Galathea crabs, starfish, sponges, rat-tail fish, anemones and other sea life that today call the wreck their home.

★

This is inside the ship. A hundred years ago, for four days, people laughed and danced here, played and exercised, courted and made love, toasted one another, sang the praises of their captain, drank to his good health and his continued success. Many of them dreamt, as they looked out over the beautiful North Atlantic, of what was to come. For them—for many of them—their time in this earthly realm would be short. Because of their ill fate, future ships would be dripping with lifeboats, and midnight runs through the ice field would be approached differently if at all. Memorials to the victims would rise everywhere: Harvard University; Washington, D.C.; four separate commemorations in Southampton, England (one each for the firemen and crew, the musicians, the postal officers and the engineers) and, of course, in the three cemeteries in Halifax. The people would be commemorated, and the other ships that played a role would sail on to different outcomes. The *Titanic*'s sister, the *Olympic*, would, as we mentioned much earlier, enjoy a long career, including a stint in the British Navy in World War I. The *Carpathia*, which did all she could for the *Titanic*, and the *Californian*, which perhaps didn't, would both be drafted into military service as well, and both would be sunk by German U-boats during the war—luckily, with the loss of only six lives. So the people and ships that survived progressed to another fate, and those who died with the *Titanic* had their stories told and retold. One hundred years on, they are told another time. The whole of it is an epic tale having narrative and moral advantage over mere lore or legend: It has the considerable advantage, as Plato once observed when teaching on a different subject at the Academy, of being true.

★

JUST
ONE MORE

⭐

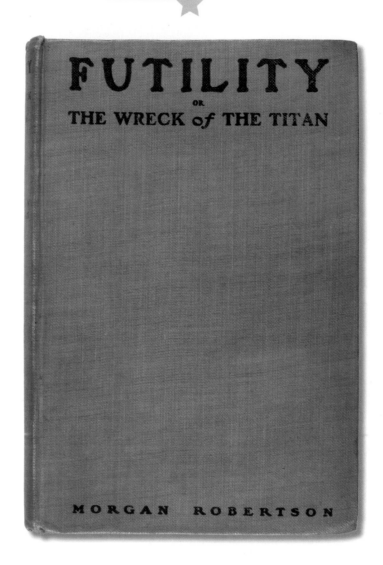

We have read by now a hundred things that seem altogether too strange to be true; this is part of the *Titanic*'s enduring hold on us: Hers is both a terrible story and a romance beyond imagining. Or is it "beyond imagining"? We have read on page 113 that the eminent British journalist (and spiritualist) William Thomas Stead, who died during the sinking, wrote a fictional sketch in the 1880s about a boat that went down in the Atlantic with a great loss of life due to too few lifeboats. Well, he also wrote, in 1892, a story about the fictional *Majestic*, of the White Star Line, traveling east to west across the ocean and picking up survivors from a ship that had hit an iceberg. So he put two major aspects together. Much earlier, in 1874, the American poet Celia Thaxter had published a volume that included "A Tryst," which passionately described a ship perishing after striking an iceberg at night, with all on board lost: "She rushed upon her ruin. Not a flash / Broke up the waiting dark; / Dully through wind and sea one awful crash / Sounded, with none to mark. / Scarcely her crew had time to clutch despair . . ." Was the American novelist and short-story writer Morgan Robertson familiar with the works of Stead or Thaxter or both? Perhaps, but no matter; his 1898 short novel *Futility*, published a full 14 years before the *Titanic* went down, takes affairs to a truly bizarre realm. His ship, the *Titan*, was a British passenger liner 800 feet in length (*Titanic* was 882.75), three propellers, same top speed as the *Titanic*, with a capacity of 3,000, said to be unsinkable. She struck an iceberg with her starboard side and went down; many passengers perished because the *Titan* carried only 24 lifeboats (just four more than the *Titanic*). The writer Robertson might have owed a debt to Stead or Thaxter, or he might have owed that debt to someone else; he claimed to be a psychic who plotted his tales with the aid of an "astral writing partner." This can be doubted, of course, but his novella exists. And so does Stead's postscript to his story from the 1880s: "This is exactly what *might* take place and *will* take place if the liners are sent to sea short of boats."